Pasta & Pizza *Presto*

Pasta & Pizza *Presto*

LORENZ BOOKS
NEW YORK • LONDON • SYDNEY • BATH

This edition first published in 1996 by Lorenz Books
27 West 20th Street, New York, NY 10011

LORENZ BOOKS are available for bulk purchase for sales promotion
and for premium use. For details, write or call the sales director,
Lorenz Books, 27 West 20th Street, New York, NY 10011; (800) 354-9657

ISBN 1 85967 279 5

Contributing authors: Maxine Clarke, Shirley Gill,
Sue Maggs, Annie Nichols and Steven Wheeler
Publisher: Joanna Lorenz
Senior Cookery Editor: Linda Fraser
Assistant Editor: Emma Brown
Designer: Siân Keogh
Photographers: James Duncan, Karl Adamson and Edward Allwright
Stylists: Madeleine Brehaut and Hilary Guy

Printed in Hong Kong / China

The material in this book previously appeared as individual titles in the *Step-by-Step* series.

3 5 7 9 10 8 6 4

CONTENTS

INTRODUCTION

Pasta and pizzas are two of the greatest highlights of Italian cuisine. Not only are they absolutely delicious and infinitely varied, they are also cheap, filling, nutritious and quick and easy to prepare. *Pasta & Pizza Presto* brings together some of the most authentic recipes, carefully selected for their diversity and the ease and speed with which they can be prepared. With minimal effort, you can quickly and simply prepare a stunning pasta or pizza dish – just follow one of these straightforward, step-by-step recipes and impress your friends with the fabulous results.

The recipes contained in this volume include such timeless classics as Spaghetti alla Carbonara and Quattro Stagioni Pizza. Vegetarians are well catered for, with a large selection of meat-free pasta and pizza dishes, as are the more carnivorous – Tagliatelle with Prosciutto and Parmesan, and Spicy Sausage Pizza are sure to delight. Fish dishes are also well represented, and for those with a sweet tooth, the highly innovative chapter of sweet pasta dishes is a must.

One of the best features of both pasta and pizza is their flexibility. By adjusting the size of the portions you serve, many of these recipes can be used as both appetizers and main courses, and several of the pasta salads and pizzas are ideal buffet fare. Pizza toppings can be used on bases of any size – why not use your favorite topping on small, individual bases for a tasty appetizer or light lunch, or on mini bases for canapés and finger foods?

For all lovers of pasta and pizzas this book is an essential, and for anyone less familiar with this marvelous food the recipes included here provide the best possible introduction. Buon appetito!

Herbs and Spices

Herbs and spices are essential for seasoning pasta dishes and pizzas and improving their flavor. Fresh herbs should be used whenever possible. Buy growing herbs in pots if you can: this ensures the herbs are as fresh as possible and provides a continuous supply.

Basil
Intensely aromatic, basil has a distinctive peppery flavor. The leaves can be used to garnish pizzas and are also ideal as a main seasoning ingredient. Traditional basil pesto is the perfect partner for pasta.

Black peppercorns
Black peppercorns are best used freshly ground in a mill or crushed as the taste and aroma disappears quickly.

Chilies (fresh and dried chili products)
Fresh chilies vary in taste, from mild to fiery hot. Generally the large, round fleshy varieties are milder than the small, thin-skinned pointed ones. For a milder, spicy flavor, remove the seeds and veins.

Red chili flakes are made from dried, crushed chilies and are somewhat milder than fresh chilies. They can be heated with olive oil to make chili oil for brushing over pizza bases or used to add bite to pizza toppings and pasta sauces.

Mild chili powder is a commercially prepared mixture of chili, ground herbs and spices. It can be used to flavor more contemporary-style dishes.

Chives
A member of the onion family, the long, narrow green leaves can be used as a garnish or snipped and added to a pasta sauce or pizza dough.

Cilantro
The delicate light green leaves have an unusual flavor and distinctive aroma. Chopped leaves are sometimes used in Californian-style pizzas and to flavor pasta dough. The fresh leaves also make an attractive garnish.

Cumin
These seeds have a warm, earthy flavor and aromatic fragrance and are sold whole or ground. Use in pasta dishes and pizzas, especially those with chili and oregano, for a Mexican flavor.

Curly parsley
This provides color and gives a fresh, clean flavor.

Italian parsley
This variety has much more flavor than common curly parsley, but they can be used interchangeably.

Herbes de Provence
A dried herb mixture of thyme, savory, rosemary, marjoram and oregano. It is especially good added to pasta and pizza doughs or sprinkled over pizzas before they are cooked.

Nutmeg
Nutmeg has a sweetish, highly aromatic flavor which has an affinity for rich foods. It is used to great effect in stuffed pizzas, pizza toppings, and cheesy pasta dishes.

Oregano
An aromatic and highly flavored herb, oregano features very strongly in Italian cooking, where it perfectly complements tomato-based sauces.

Rosemary
Rosemary, with its pungent, dark green, needle-like leaves, can be overpowering, but when used judiciously, it can add a delicious flavor to vegetables for an unusual, aromatic pasta sauce or pizza topping.

Saffron
The dried stigmas of the saffron crocus, saffron is the most expensive spice in the world, but fortunately very little is needed in most recipes, sometimes as little as a pinch. Pungent with a brilliant yellow color, saffron is available as strands or ground.

Sage
Just a few leaves can deliciously flavor a sauce or topping, especially with a rich-tasting cheese like Gorgonzola; sage tends to overpower subtle flavors.

Salt
For seasoning, use sea salt flakes or refined table salt; the former has a slightly stronger flavor so use it sparingly. Salt also balances the action of yeast and is an integral part of making bread, and hence pizza dough.

Thyme
This is excellent chopped or crumbled, and stirred into tomato sauces or sprinkled on to pasta and pizza dishes. Whole sprigs can be used as a garnish.

saffron

red chili flakes

cilantro

mild chili powder

fresh red chilies

chives

thyme

curly parsley

Italian parsley

ground cumin

herbes de Provence

nutmeg

sage

rosemary

oregano

basil

black peppercorns

sea salt

Fresh Vegetables

Never has vegetable cooking been so exciting. A quick glance in the greengrocer's and supermarket reveals a remarkable choice. There are baby eggplant, wild mushrooms, red onions, colorful peppers, hot-tasting chilies, as well as fennel and wonderful asparagus – a truly international offering, providing endless possibilities to the cook.

As vegetables are so full of color they make attractive and tempting pasta sauces and pizza toppings. Choose the best quality fresh vegetables for maximum flavor and scout around to see what is newly in season. Try Tagliatelle with Pea Sauce, Asparagus and Broad Beans, or Eggplant, Shallot and Sun-dried Tomato Calzone, or invent your own combinations. Vegetable dishes are not just for vegetarians; they are for everyone who enjoys exciting food, inventively prepared and presented with style.

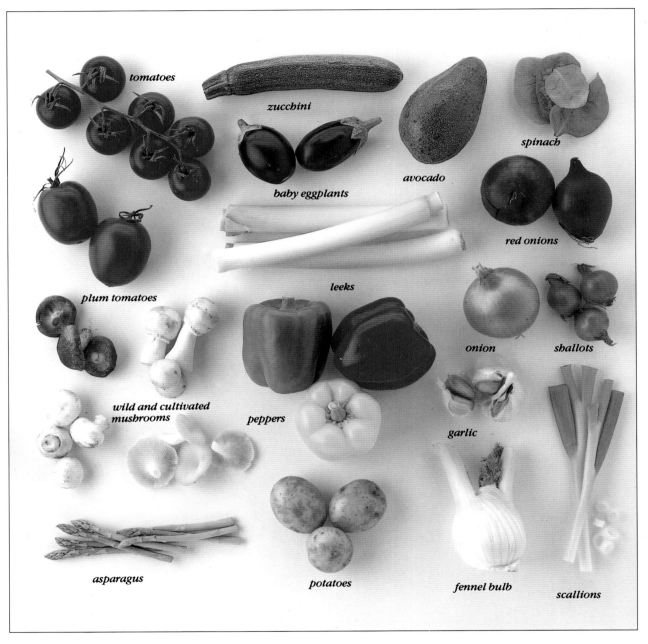

tomatoes

zucchini

baby eggplants

avocado

spinach

plum tomatoes

leeks

red onions

onion

shallots

wild and cultivated mushrooms

peppers

garlic

asparagus

potatoes

fennel bulb

scallions

Meat and Fish

Pasta or pizzas with a meat or fish sauce or topping make a marvelous substantial lunch or supper dish served with tossed salad leaves. A wealth of delicious ingredients can be used. Sliced cured meats, salamis, ham and sausages are perennial favorites. Look for them in supermarkets where they may be either pre-packed in the meat section or at the delicatessen counter. Chicken and ground beef can also be used in many varied and highly imaginative ways.

Fresh fish and shellfish also make tempting sauces and toppings. Favorites such as shrimp, mussels, squid and salmon may be used alone or mixed for a good variety of flavors. Canned fish such as tuna and anchovies are also important. If you find anchovies too salty, it helps to soak them in milk before use. For best results, ensure that fish and shellfish are not overcooked or the flavor may be spoiled. When you are shopping for fish and shellfish the most important quality to look for is, of course, freshness.

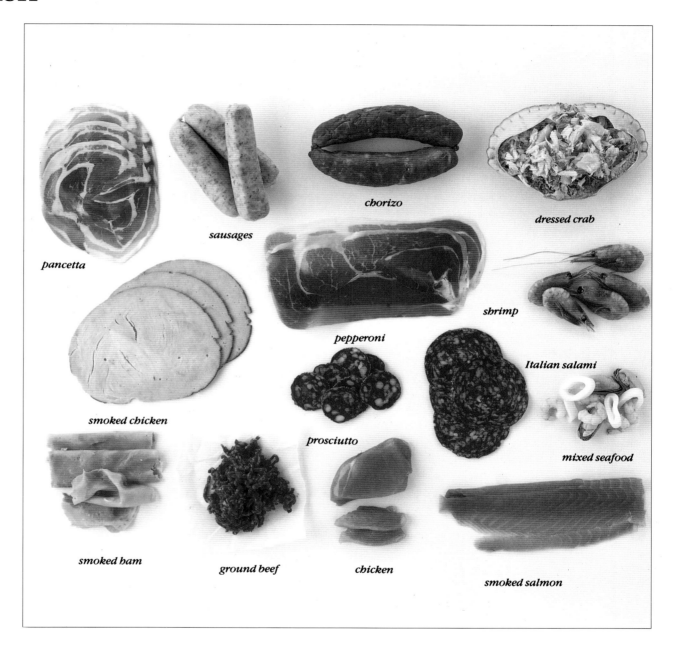

sausages

chorizo

dressed crab

pancetta

shrimp

pepperoni

Italian salami

smoked chicken

prosciutto

mixed seafood

smoked ham

ground beef

chicken

smoked salmon

Pantry Cupboard

For the most part the recipes in this book call upon fresh everyday ingredients and certain essential items from the pantry cupboard. There are a few special ingredients, however, which are worth hunting for. They may seem expensive, but just a little will go a long way to give your dishes character and flair.

Anchovies
Canned anchovies imported from the Mediterranean have been filleted and salted before being packed in oil. They are an important flavoring ingredient and garnish.

Artichoke hearts
When these are specified in a recipe, those packed in oil in jars have been used unless stated otherwise.

Capers
These are the flower buds of a shrub native to the Mediterranean which are preserved in vinegar and salt or salt alone. They have a strong piquant flavor and should be used with care.

Cornmeal (polenta)
Adds texture and an earthy flavor to a basic pizza dough.

Flour
White flour contains 72–74 per cent of the wheat grain. It is available in all-purpose, bread and self-rising forms.

Traditional pizza bases are made from bread dough, which is usually made with white bread flour. This flour has a high gluten content. Pasta dough can also be made with white bread flour.

All-purpose white flour is commonly used to make pasta dough. It is also used to make focaccia, a flattish bread with a variety of different toppings.

Self-rising white flour has had leavening or raising agents added to it, and is suitable for a scone pizza base.

Whole-wheat flour is simply flour milled from the whole grain with nothing added or taken away. It is used to make brown, whole-wheat pasta. Bread and self-rising whole-wheat flours are used for making pizza doughs. For a lighter result, try mixing whole-wheat with white flour.

Olives
Green olives are unripe; black are fully ripe and have more flavor. They are widely available in many forms – whole or pitted, or stuffed with ingredients like pimientoes or anchovy fillets. You can buy them preserved in brine or oil, and they are used only in their preserved state. Pitted olives can be used in pasta sauces and to garnish pizzas.

Olive oil
A "pure" olive oil of good quality is indispensable for making traditional Italian food. Ingredients such as garlic and chilies can be added to the oil to provide extra flavor. Extra virgin olive oil is usually a darker green and has a more intense flavor. It is well worth buying good quality olive oil – look for oils which are cold pressed.

Pimiento
Pimiento is the Spanish word for pepper. The red variety is available packed whole into cans. Sweet flavored, with a bright red color, they are a very useful pantry cupboard standby.

Pine nuts
These small, oval, creamy colored nuts with a sweet flavor are much appreciated in the Mediterranean and Middle East. They may be sprinkled over pasta or on to pizzas to add a crunchy texture, or used freshly ground in sauces such as pesto.

Rapid-rise dried yeast
Much faster and quicker to use than fresh or dried yeast, as its name implies. It does not need to be reconstituted in liquid first, but is mixed directly with the flour. Use lukewarm liquid to mix the dough as high temperatures can kill the yeast and the dough will not rise.

Red pesto
A richly aromatic sauce combining pesto with sun-dried tomatoes. Red pesto is delicious spread on to pizza bases, stirred into tomato sauces or simply served alone as a topping to freshly cooked pasta.

Sun-dried tomato paste
This has a richer, more intense flavor than ordinary tomato paste and makes a quick pizza topping. It also enriches sauces and gives a lovely color.

Tapenade
This is made from green or black olives ground to a paste with a little olive oil and seasoning. Delicious tossed with pasta or spread on to pizza bases, it is especially good with dishes containing goat cheese.

Tomatoes: canned
An essential – no pantry cupboard should be without them! Canned tomatoes come either whole or crushed, ready for use in sauces and toppings.

Tomatoes: sun-dried in oil
Sun-dried tomatoes have a concentrated, salty flavor, which is excellent used in small quantities in breads and as a pasta or pizza topping. They can also be bought loose in their dry state but they will need to be soaked in warm water before use.

Tomato paste
Useful for adding color, intensity and flavor to homemade tomato-based sauces.

Tuna
Canned tuna fish is usually packed in oil, brine or water. Its firm texture makes it a versatile and useful ingredient.

Walnuts
Walnuts can be used to make delicious breads and pasta sauces.

anchovies

pimiento

walnuts

olive oil

sun-dried tomatoes

tuna

pine nuts

canned tomatoes

sun-dried tomato paste

artichoke hearts

capers

cornmeal

tomato paste

red pesto

black olives

green olives

rapid-rise dried yeast

plain flour

black olive tapenade

green olive tapenade

whole wheat flour

bread flour

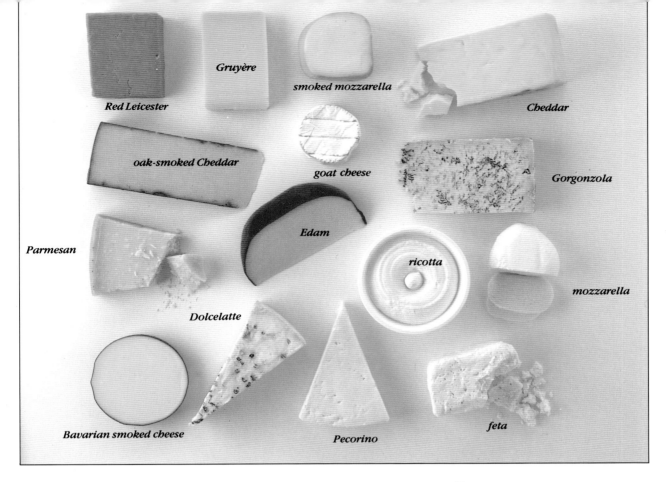

Red Leicester

Gruyère

smoked mozzarella

Cheddar

oak-smoked Cheddar

goat cheese

Gorgonzola

Parmesan

Edam

ricotta

mozzarella

Dolcelatte

Bavarian smoked cheese

Pecorino

feta

Cheeses

One of the most important elements in the making of a tasty pizza or cheese-based pasta dish is the cheese. A variety of cheeses can be used, so experiment with different ones to suit your taste and to best complement the other ingredients.

Bavarian smoked cheese
Sold in rounds with a brown wax coating, this cheese has a pale creamy color and mild, smoky flavor, with a texture that is smooth and soft.

Cheddar
This cow's milk cheese is produced commercially but also by small dairy farmers. Flavours can vary from mild to quite strong. It is a very versatile cheese, which is ideal for cooking with since it doesn't draw threads. Cheddar is universally popular.

Dolcelatte
An Italian blue-veined, semi-soft cheese. It has a smooth, creamy texture and delicate piquant flavor.

Edam
A Dutch ball-shaped cheese, firm and smooth in texture with a mild, nutty flavor.

Feta
Feta is a fairly hard cheese that crumbles easily. It is preserved in brine which accounts for its salty flavor – rinse it well before use. Feta can also sometimes be bought in oil; make sure it is well drained before use.

Goat cheese
Goat cheeses are small, generally shaped in logs, rounds, pyramids or ovals, and range in flavor from fresh and creamy to strong, dry and tangy. They cook well and are especially good with roasted vegetables for a delicious-tasting vegetarian dish.

Gorgonzola *piccante*
This cheese is pleasantly sharp in flavor, with a softish texture and blue-green veins.

Gruyère
A hard cheese with a distinctive sweet and nutty taste, it is widely used in cooking as it has good melting properties.

Mozzarella
This versatile cheese is used in many pizza recipes for its astounding melting quality. It is also excellent in pasta salads.

Oak-smoked Cheddar
A Cheddar variant which adds a distinctive smoky flavor and cooks well.

Parmesan
Italy's most famous hard cheese, which is usually grated for cooking and serving with pasta and pizzas. Always buy fresh Parmesan if you can, as it is by far the best.

Pecorino
An Italian sheep's cheese which has a fairly strong distinctive flavor. It is used in the same way as Parmesan.

Red Leicester
This cheese has a mild flavor and bright color.

Ricotta
A soft Italian whey cheese with a delicate, smooth flavor. It is ideal for use in fillings for calzone and for baked pasta dishes.

Smoked mozzarella
Smoked mozzarella has a creamy, smoky taste that gives it a more distinctive flavor than the plain variety. It also has excellent melting properties.

salt and pepper mills
pizza pans
jelly-roll pan
bowls
flour sifter
measuring cup
oil can
box grater
nutmeg grater
pastry brush
baking sheet
Parmesan grater
rolling pin
wooden spoon
pizza wheels
pizza stone
cook's knife
olive pitter
pastry cutter
metal spoons
garlic press
measuring spoons
pizza cutter
vegetable knife

Equipment for Pizzas

To make pizzas successfully you do not have to have special tools, but tasks are made simpler with the aid of certain utensils and gadgets.

Baking sheet
Choose a large heavy baking sheet that will not warp at high temperatures.

Bowls
A set of bowls in various sizes is essential when cooking.

Box grater
A multi-surface grater can be used for all grating purposes.

Cook's knife
This has a heavy, wide blade ideal for chopping.

Flour sifter
A useful piece of equipment for dusting the work surface.

Garlic press
This is a small metal gadget used for crushing garlic.

Jelly-roll pan
A rectangular pan, ideal for making hearty farmhouse pizzas.

Measuring cup
Essential for measuring liquid, these cups are available in a wide range of sizes.

Measuring spoons
For accurately measuring small amounts of ingredients.

Metal spoons
The best metal spoons are oval with a pointed end.

Nutmeg grater
This is a miniature grater used for grating whole nutmegs.

Olive oil can
Usually made of metal, it has a long, narrow spout for drizzling oil on to pizzas.

Olive pitter
This removes pits from olives with one quick press.

Parmesan grater
A special grater for Parmesan.

Pastry brush
This is useful for brushing on oil, water or beaten egg white.

Pastry cutter
This is used for stamping out dough rounds.

Pizza cutter/lifter
A dual-purpose gadget for cutting and serving pizzas.

Pizza pan
Traditional pizza pans are round and shallow. Deep-dish pizza pans are also available, but a square cake pan may be used instead. A perforated pizza pan allows steam to escape and encourages the base to crispen.

Pizza stone
A terracotta round, used instead of a baking sheet or pizza pan. The stone absorbs and retains heat, and crisps the dough.

Pizza wheel
This large cutting wheel is useful for easy slicing.

Rolling pin
Choose a long, heavy pin to ensure even rolling.

Salt and pepper mills
These are used specifically for grinding coarse sea salt and whole peppercorns.

Vegetable knife
A small knife for trimming and peeling vegetables.

Wooden spoons
Essential in all kitchens is a set of wooden spoons.

Equipment for Pasta

Only a clean table top and a rolling pin are necessary to make pasta, but there are a number of gadgets available which make pasta making easier.

Bowls
A set of bowls is useful for mixing, whisking and so on.

Chopping board
A hygienic nylon board is best for cutting and chopping.

Colander
A large colander is essential for draining cooked pasta quickly.

Cook's knife
Use an all-purpose cook's knife for cutting pasta and chopping.

Flour sifter
Useful for dusting pasta with small amounts of flour.

Large metal spoon
For folding in and serving sauces.

Measuring spoons
For accurately measuring small quantities of ingredients.

Pasta machine or roller
Useful for kneading, rolling and cutting pasta – a real labor-saver.

Pasta or pastry wheel
For cutting pasta, such as pasta bows, with a decorated edge.

Pastry brush
For removing excess flour from pasta and for brushing pasta with water, milk or beaten egg to seal.

Perforated spoon
Useful for draining small amounts of food.

Pestle and mortar
For hand-grinding pesto and crushing black peppercorns.

Ravioli cutter
For cutting or stamping out individual raviolis; can be round or square. A selection of pastry cutters can also be used.

Ravioli tray (raviolatore)
For making sheets of ravioli quickly and neatly – with practice!

Rolling pin
Pasta pins are available in some kitchenware stores – they are long, thin and tapered at each end. However an ordinary heavy wooden rolling pin will do.

Small grater
For freshly grating nutmeg and Parmesan cheese.

Vegetable knife
For preparing vegetables, paring lemons, and for delicate work.

Vegetable peeler
For shaving Parmesan cheese.

Whisk
Essential for beating eggs and combining sauces smoothly.

bowls

pasta machine

cook's knife

measuring spoons

sifter

rolling pin

pestle and mortar

cutters

colander

perforated spoon

large metal spoon

chopping board

vegetable knife

pastry brush

vegetable peeler

metal whisk

pastry wheel

small grater

ravioli cutter

ravioli tray

PASTA PRESTO

Pasta has rapidly become one of today's staple foods, traveling across the world in various forms from Asia to South America. Its origins are unclear, but a type of pasta was certainly made in Sicily, the grain store of Rome, in the days of the Roman Empire. It has also existed in China and Japan for many centuries, but in very different forms and shapes.

The enormous popularity of pasta is due to its incredible versatility, its value for money and the ease and speed with which it can be used to make a satisfying meal. You can produce sauces in next to no time with small amounts of meat or fish, mix them with pasta and produce a filling and nutritious dish. Most wheat-flour-and-water (commercial dried) pasta contains more proteins and carbohydrates than potatoes, so when combined with a sauce of vegetables, cheese or meat, it gives a good nutritional balance. It is a fine source of energy too – better than sugar, as it releases energy at a slower prolonged rate, and will give you a lift if you are tired and hungry. Pasta is only fattening if eaten in over-large quantities with too much sauce! Italians fill up on the pasta itself, the sauce being an adornment to enhance the flavor.

Pasta is very easy to make at home if you have patience and a little time to spare. The result is exciting and delicious, and once you have mastered the technique you can make one of life's staples. Fresh egg pasta is made only with wheat flour, eggs, a little salt and olive oil and it freezes well. Freeze it in batches and use as required to make tasty, healthy meals, presto!

Pasta Types

When buying dried pasta, choose good-quality well-known brands. Of the 'fresh' pasta sold in sealed packs in supermarkets, the filled or stuffed varieties are worth buying; noodles and ribbon pasta are better bought dried, as these tend to have more bite when cooked. However, if you are lucky enough to live near an Italian grocer, where pasta is made on the premises, it will usually be of very good quality. Fresh is not necessarily better, but the final choice is yours — the best pasta is homemade, as you can then be sure of the quality of the ingredients used and also of the finished texture.

You will see from this book that the sauces are almost limitless in their variety, as are the pasta shapes themselves. There are no hard-and-fast rules regarding which shape to use with which pasta sauce: it's really a matter of personal preference. However, there are a few guidelines to follow, such as that thin spaghetti suits seafood sauces, thicker spaghetti is good with creamy sauces (as in, for instance, Spaghetti alla Carbonara) and thick tubular pasta, like rigatoni, penne and so on, suits rustic sauces full of bits that will be caught in the pasta itself.

macaroni

vermicelli

quick-cook macaroni

fresh squid-ink tagliatelle

orzo or puntalette

small soup pasta

fettuccine: tomato, spinach, and plain

fresh caramellone

fettuccia riccia

fresh cappelletti

lasagne lunghe

fresh ravioli

fresh tortelloni

garganelle

'paglia e fieno'
('straw and hay' tagliarini)

fresh pappardelle

*fresh beet
tagliatelle*

*fresh wild-mushroom
tagliatelle*

spaghetti

spinach spaghetti

whole-wheat spaghetti

pipe rigate

*conchigliette rigate
(small pasta shells)*

Pasta bows
(farfalle)

campanelle

cannelloni

rigatoni

*pasta shells
(conchiglie)*

spirali

lasagne

spinach lasagne

whole-wheat shells

orecchiette

Techniques

To Cook Pasta

1 Throw the pasta into a large pan of boiling salted water. Stir once to prevent sticking. The addition of 1 tbsp vegetable or olive oil will help to stop the water boiling over and prevent the pasta from sticking. *Do not cover* the pan or the water will boil over.

2 Quickly bring the pasta back to a rolling boil and boil until *al dente* (literally 'to the tooth') – the pasta should be just firm to the bite. It should not have a hard center or be very floppy.

3 Quickly drain the pasta well, using a large colander or strainer. Immediately rinse the pasta with boiling water to wash off any starch and to prevent the pasta from sticking together. At this stage you can toss the pasta in a little olive oil or butter if not dressing with the sauce immediately. Serve hot pasta straight away. It is up to you whether you toss the pasta with the sauce before serving or serve it with the sauce on top.

Cooking Times for Fresh and Dried Pasta

Calculate the cooking time from the moment the water returns to a boil after the pasta has been added.

Unfilled pasta
Fresh: 2–3 minutes, though some very thin pasta is ready as soon as the water returns to the boil.
Dried: 8–12 minutes, but keep checking as this is only a guide.

Filled pasta
Fresh: 8–10 minutes.
Dried: 15–20 minutes.

Basic Pasta Dough

Allow 1¾ cups all-purpose flour, a pinch of salt, and 1 tbsp olive oil to 2 eggs for 3–4 servings, depending on the required size of portion.

1 Sift the flour and salt onto a clean work surface and make a well in the center with your fist.

2 Pour the beaten eggs and oil into the well. Gradually mix the eggs into the flour with the fingers of one hand.

3 Knead the pasta until smooth, wrap, and allow to rest for at least 30 minutes before attempting to roll out. The pasta will be much more elastic after resting.

Using a Food Processor

1 Sift the flour into the bowl and add a pinch of salt.

2 Pour in the beaten eggs and oil and any chosen flavoring, and process until the dough begins to come together.

3 Tip out the dough and knead until smooth. Wrap and rest for 30 minutes. Use as required.

Using a Pasta Machine

1 Feed the rested dough several times through the highest setting first, then reducing the settings until the required thickness is achieved.

2 A special cutter will produce fettuccine or tagliatelle.

3 A narrower cutter will produce spaghetti or tagliarini.

COOK'S TIP

These are only guidelines: depending on the air humidity, the type of flour and so on, you may have to add more flour. The dough must not be too soft – it should be quite hard to knead. Too much extra flour will make the pasta tough and taste floury!

WATER NEEDED TO COOK PASTA

4½ quarts water plus 3 tbsp salt for every 11 oz–1 lb dried pasta or 11 oz–1 lb fresh pasta. This will prevent the pasta from sticking.

FLAVORED PASTA

Tomato Pasta
Add 2 tbsp tomato paste to the flour. Use about 1½ eggs.

Beet Pasta
Add 2 tbsp grated cooked beet to the flour. Use about 1½ eggs.

Saffron Pasta
Soak a packet of powdered saffron in 2 tbsp hot water for 15 minutes. Use 1½ eggs and whisk the saffron water into them.

Herb Pasta
Add 3 tbsp chopped fresh herbs to the flour.

Whole-wheat Pasta
Use 1¼ cups whole-wheat flour sifted with ¼ cup all-purpose flour and 2 eggs.

Macaroni

Macaroni is the generic name for any hollow pasta. This method is for making garganelle.

1 Cut squares of pasta dough using a sharp knife on a floured surface.

2 Wrap the squares around a pencil or chopstick on the diagonal to form tubes. Slip off and allow to dry slightly.

SPINACH PASTA

Use 5 oz frozen leaf spinach, cooked and squeezed of as much moisture as possible, a pinch of salt, 2 eggs, and about 1¾ cups all-purpose flour (the pasta may need a little more if sticky). Proceed as in the recipe for Basic Pasta Dough, but liquidize the spinach with the eggs to give a fine texture to the dough.

Tagliatelle

Tagliatelle can also be made with a pasta machine, but it is fairly straightforward to make it by hand.

1 Roll up the floured pasta dough like a jelly roll.

2 Cut the roll into thin slices with a sharp knife. Immediately unravel the slices to reveal the pasta ribbons. To make tagliarini cut the slices ⅛ in thick.

3 To make pappardelle, using a serrated pastry wheel, cut out wide ribbons from the rolled pasta dough.

Tortellini

Tortellini or 'little twists' can be made with meat or vegetarian fillings and served with sauce or in a soup.

1 Using a round cookie cutter, stamp out rounds of pasta.

2 Pipe or spoon the chosen filling into the middle of each round.

3 Brush the edges with beaten egg and fold the round into a crescent shape, excluding all the air. Bend the 2 corners round to meet each other and press well to seal. Repeat with the remaining dough. Leave to dry on a floured dish towel for 30 minutes before cooking.

SPINACH, RICOTTA, AND PARMESAN FILLING FOR STUFFED PASTA
Serves 4–6

1 lb frozen spinach, thawed and squeezed dry
½ tsp freshly grated nutmeg
1 tsp salt
freshly ground black pepper
¾ cup fresh ricotta or cottage cheese
¼ cup freshly grated Parmesan cheese

Place all the ingredients in a food processor and process until smooth. Use as required.

Ravioli

Although ravioli can be bought ready made, the very best is made at home. Serve with sauce or in a soup.

1 Cut the dough in half and wrap one portion in plastic wrap. Roll out the pasta thinly to a rectangle on a lightly floured surface. Cover with a clean damp dish towel and repeat with the remaining pasta. Pipe small mounds (about 1 tsp) of filling in even rows, spacing them at 1½ in intervals, across one piece of the dough. Brush the spaces between the filling with beaten egg.

2 Using a rolling pin, lift the remaining sheet of pasta over the dough with the filling. Press down firmly between the pockets of filling, pushing out any air.

3 Cut into squares with a serrated ravioli cutter or sharp knife. Transfer to a floured dish towel and rest for 1 hour before cooking.

Minestrone

A classic substantial winter soup originally from Milan, but found in various versions around the Mediterranean coasts of Italy and France. Cut the vegetables as roughly or as small as you like. Add freshly grated Parmesan cheese just before serving.

Serves 6–8

INGREDIENTS
2 cups dried white beans
2 tbsp olive oil
2 oz bacon, diced
2 large onions, sliced
2 garlic cloves, crushed
2 medium carrots, diced
3 celery sticks, sliced
14 oz canned chopped tomatoes
10 cups beef stock
12 oz potatoes, diced
1½ cups small pasta shapes
  (macaroni, stars, shells, etc)
½ lb green cabbage, thinly sliced
6 oz fine green beans, sliced
¾ cup frozen peas
3 tbsp chopped fresh parsley
salt and pepper
freshly grated Parmesan cheese,
  to serve

1 Cover the beans with cold water and leave to soak overnight.

2 Heat the oil in a large saucepan and add the bacon, onions, and garlic. Cover and cook gently for 5 minutes, stirring occasionally, until soft.

3 Add the carrots and celery and cook for 2–3 minutes until softening.

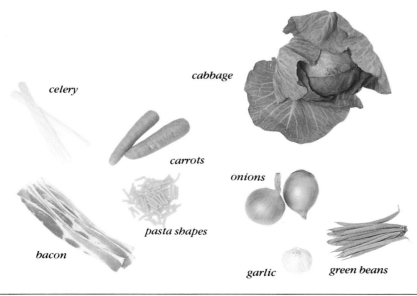

celery

cabbage

carrots

onions

pasta shapes

bacon

garlic

green beans

4 Drain the beans and add to the pan with the tomatoes and stock. Cover and simmer for 2–2½ hours, until the beans are tender.

5 Add the potatoes 30 minutes before the soup is finished.

VARIATION

To make Soupe au Pistou from the South of France, stir in a basil, garlic and pine nut sauce (pesto or pistou) just before serving.

6 Add the pasta, cabbage, beans, peas, and parsley 15 minutes before the soup is ready. Season to taste and serve with a bowl of freshly grated Parmesan cheese.

Italian Bean and Pasta Soup

A thick and hearty soup which, followed by bread and cheese, makes a substantial lunch.

Serves 6

INGREDIENTS
1½ cups dried white beans, soaked overnight in cold water
7½ cups chicken stock or water
1 cup medium pasta shells
4 tbsp olive oil, plus extra to serve
2 garlic cloves, crushed
4 tbsp chopped fresh parsley
salt and pepper

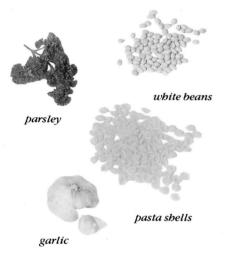

parsley

white beans

pasta shells

garlic

1 Drain the beans and place in a large saucepan with the stock or water. Simmer, half-covered, for 2–2½ hours or until tender.

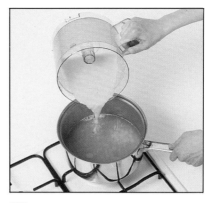

2 Liquidize half the beans and a little of their cooking liquid, then stir into the remaining beans in the pan.

3 Add the pasta and simmer gently for 15 minutes until tender. (Add extra water or stock if the soup seems too thick.)

4 Heat the oil in a small pan and fry the garlic until golden. Stir into the soup with the parsley and season well with salt and pepper. Ladle into individual bowls and drizzle each with a little extra olive oil.

Zucchini Soup with Small Pasta Shells

A pretty, fresh-tasting soup which could be made using cucumber instead of zucchini.

Serves 4–6

INGREDIENTS
4 tbsp olive or sunflower oil
2 medium onions, finely chopped
6¼ cups chicken stock
2 lb zucchini
1 cup small soup pasta
fresh lemon juice
salt and pepper
2 tbsp chopped fresh chervil
sour cream, to serve

zucchini

onion

soup pasta

chervil

1 Heat the oil in a large saucepan and add the onions. Cover and cook gently for about 20 minutes until very soft but not colored, stirring occasionally.

2 Add the stock and bring to the boil.

3 Meanwhile grate the zucchini and stir into the boiling stock with the pasta. Turn down the heat and simmer for 15 minutes until the pasta is tender. Season to taste with lemon juice, salt, and pepper.

4 Stir in the chervil and add a swirl of sour cream before serving.

COOK'S TIP
If no fresh stock is available, instead of using a stock cube, use canned chicken or beef consommé.

Provençal Fish Soup with Pasta

This colorful soup has all the flavors of the Mediterranean. Serve it as a main course for a deliciously filling lunch.

Serves 4

INGREDIENTS
2 tbsp olive oil
1 medium onion, sliced
1 garlic clove, crushed
1 leek, sliced
8 oz canned chopped tomatoes
pinch of herbes de Provence
¼ tsp saffron threads (optional)
1 cup small pasta
salt and pepper
about 8 live mussels
1 lb filleted and skinned white fish
    (cod, plaice, monkfish)

ROUILLE
2 garlic cloves, crushed
1 canned pimento, drained and
    chopped
1 tbsp fresh white bread crumbs
4 tbsp mayonnaise
toasted French bread, to serve

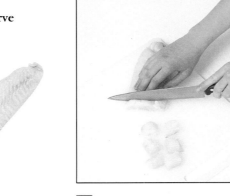

pasta

white fish

garlic

onion

mussels

leek

1 Heat the oil in a large saucepan and add the onion, garlic, and leek. Cover and cook gently for 5 minutes, stirring occasionally until soft.

2 Pour in 4½ cups water, the tomatoes, herbs, saffron, and pasta. Season with salt and pepper and cook for 15–20 minutes.

3 Scrub the mussels and pull off the 'beards'. Discard any that will not close when sharply tapped: they are almost certainly dead.

4 Cut the fish into bite-sized chunks and add to the soup, placing the mussels on top. Simmer with the lid on for 5–10 minutes until the mussels open and the fish is just cooked. (If any mussels fail to open, discard them.)

5 To make the *rouille*, pound the garlic, canned pimento, and bread crumbs together in a pestle and mortar (or in a food processor). Stir in the mayonnaise and season well.

6 Spread the toasted French bread with the *rouille* and serve with the soup.

Chicken Vermicelli Soup with Egg Shreds

This soup is very quick and easy — you can add all sorts of extra ingredients to vary the taste, using up lurking leftovers such as scallions, mushrooms, a few shrimp, chopped salami and so on.

Serves 4–6

INGREDIENTS
3 large eggs
2 tbsp chopped fresh cilantro or
   parsley
6¼ cups good chicken stock or
   canned consommé
1 cup dried vermicelli or angel hair
   pasta
¼ lb cooked chicken breast, sliced
salt and pepper

vermicelli

chicken breast

eggs

cilantro

THAI CHICKEN SOUP

To make a Thai variation, use Chinese rice noodles instead of pasta. Stir ½ tsp dried lemon grass, 2 small whole fresh chilies and 4 tbsp coconut milk into the stock. Add 4 sliced scallions and plenty of chopped fresh cilantro.

1 First make the egg shreds. Whisk the eggs together in a small bowl and stir in the cilantro or parsley.

2 Heat a small nonstick skillet and pour in 2–3 tbsp egg, swirling to cover the base evenly. Cook until set. Repeat until all the mixture is used up.

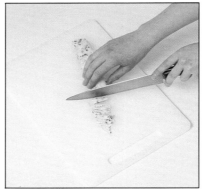

3 Roll each pancake up and slice thinly into shreds. Set aside.

4 Bring the stock to a boil and add the pasta, breaking it up into short lengths. Cook for 3–5 minutes until the pasta is almost tender, then add the chicken, salt, and pepper. Heat through for 2–3 minutes, then stir in the egg shreds. Serve immediately.

Creamy Parmesan and Cauliflower Soup with Pasta Bows

A silky smooth, mildly cheesy soup that isn't overpowered by the cauliflower. It is an elegant dinner party soup served with the crisp melba toast.

Serves 6

INGREDIENTS
1 large cauliflower
5 cups chicken or vegetable stock
1½ cups pasta bows (farfalle)
⅔ cup light cream or milk
freshly grated nutmeg
pinch of cayenne pepper
4 tbsp freshly grated Parmesan cheese
salt and pepper

MELBA TOAST
3–4 slices day-old white bread
freshly grated Parmesan cheese, for
    sprinkling
¼ tsp paprika

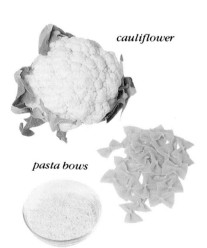
cauliflower

pasta bows

Parmesan cheese

nutmeg

1 Cut the leaves and central stalk away from the cauliflower and discard. Divide the cauliflower into florets.

2 Bring the stock to a boil and add the cauliflower. Simmer for about 10 minutes or until very soft. Remove the cauliflower with a perforated spoon and place in a food processor.

3 Add the pasta to the stock and simmer for 10 minutes until tender. Drain, reserve the pasta, and pour the liquid over the cauliflower in the food processor. Add the cream or milk, nutmeg, and cayenne to the cauliflower. Blend until smooth, then press through a strainer. Stir in the cooked pasta. Reheat the soup and stir in the Parmesan. Taste and adjust the seasoning.

4 Meanwhile make the melba toast. Preheat the oven to 350°F. Toast the bread lightly on both sides. Quickly cut off the crusts and split each slice in half horizontally. Scrape off any doughy bits and sprinkle with Parmesan and paprika. Place on a baking sheet and bake in the oven for 10–15 minutes or until uniformly golden. Serve with the soup.

Pasta with Roasted Bell Pepper and Tomato Sauce

Add other vegetables such as French beans or zucchini or even chick peas (garbanzos) to make this sauce more substantial.

Serves 4

INGREDIENTS
2 medium red bell peppers
2 medium yellow bell peppers
3 tbsp olive oil
1 medium onion, sliced
2 garlic cloves, crushed
½ tsp mild chili powder
14 oz canned chopped plum tomatoes
salt and pepper
4 cups dried pasta shells or spirals
freshly grated Parmesan cheese, to
    serve

bell peppers

pasta shells

onion

garlic

1 Preheat the oven to 400°F. Place the bell peppers on a baking sheet or in a roasting pan and bake for about 20 minutes or until beginning to char. Alternatively broil the peppers, turning frequently.

2 Rub the skins off the peppers under cold water. Halve, remove the seeds, and roughly chop the flesh.

3 Heat the oil in a medium saucepan and add the onion and garlic. Cook gently for 5 minutes until soft and golden.

4 Stir in the chili powder, cook for 2 minutes, then add the tomatoes and peppers. Bring to a boil and simmer for 10–15 minutes until slightly thickened and reduced. Season to taste.

5 Cook the pasta in plenty of boiling salted water according to the manufacturer's instructions. Drain well and toss with the sauce. Serve piping hot with lots of Parmesan cheese.

Coriander Ravioli with Pumpkin filling

A stunning herb pasta with a superb creamy pumpkin and roast garlic filling.

Serves 4–6

INGREDIENTS
scant 1 cup flour
2 eggs
pinch of salt
3 tbsp chopped fresh coriander
coriander sprigs, to garnish

FOR THE FILLING
4 garlic cloves in their skins
1 lb pumpkin, peeled and seeds
   removed
½ cup ricotta cheese
4 halves sun-dried tomatoes in olive
   oil, drained and finely chopped, but
   reserve 2 tbsp of the oil
freshly ground black pepper

coriander

pumpkin

egg

garlic

flour

ricotta
cheese

sun-dried tomatoes

1 Place the flour, eggs, salt and coriancer into a food processor. Pulse until combined.

2 Place the dough on a lightly floured board and knead well for 5 minutes, until smooth. Wrap in plastic wrap and leave to rest in the fridge for 20 minutes.

3 Preheat the oven to 400°F. Place the garlic cloves on a cookie sheet and bake for 10 minutes until softened. Steam the pumpkin for 5–8 minutes until tender and drain well. Peel the garlic cloves and mash into the pumpkin together with the ricotta and drained sun-dried tomatoes. Season with black pepper.

4 Divide the pasta into 4 pieces and flatten slightly. Using a pasta machine, on its thinnest setting, roll out each piece. Leave the sheets of pasta on a clean dish-towel until slightly dried.

5 Using a 3 in crinkle-edged round cutter, stamp out 36 rounds.

6 Top 18 of the rounds with a teaspoonful of mixture, brush the edges with water and place another round of pasta on top. Press firmly around the edges to seal. Bring a large pan of water to a boil, add the ravioli and cook for 3–4 minutes. Drain well and toss into the reserved tomato oil. Serve garnished with coriander sprigs.

Tagliatelle with Walnut Sauce

An unusual sauce that would make this a spectacular dinner party starter.

Serves 4–6

INGREDIENTS
2 thick slices whole-wheat bread
1¼ cups milk
2½ cups walnut pieces
1 garlic clove, crushed
½ cup freshly grated Parmesan cheese
6 tbsp olive oil, plus extra for tossing the pasta
salt and pepper
⅓ cup heavy cream (optional)
1 lb tagliatelle
2 tbsp chopped fresh parsley

1 Cut the crusts off the bread and soak in the milk until the milk is all absorbed.

2 Preheat the oven to 375°F. Spread the walnuts on a baking sheet and toast in the oven for 5 minutes. Leave to cool.

3 Place the bread, walnuts, garlic, Parmesan cheese, and olive oil in a food processor and blend until smooth. Season to taste with salt and pepper. Stir in the cream, if using.

tagliatelle

parsley

garlic

walnut pieces

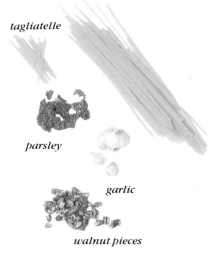

VARIATION

Add ¾ cup pitted black olives to the food processor with the other ingredients for a richer, more piquant sauce. The Greek-style olives have the most flavor.

4 Cook the pasta in plenty of boiling salted water, drain, and toss with a little olive oil. Divide the pasta equally between 4 bowls and place a dollop of sauce on each portion. Sprinkle liberally with parsley.

Stir-fried Vegetables with Pasta

This is a colorful Chinese-style dish, easily prepared using pasta instead of Chinese noodles.

Serves 4

INGREDIENTS
1 medium carrot
6 oz small zucchini
6 oz green beans
6 oz baby corn
1 lb ribbon pasta such as tagliatelle
salt
2 tbsp corn oil, plus extra for tossing the pasta
½ in piece fresh ginger, peeled and finely chopped
2 garlic cloves, finely chopped
6 tbsp yellow bean sauce
6 scallions, sliced into 1 in lengths
2 tbsp dry sherry
1 tsp sesame seeds

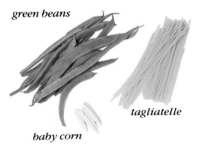
green beans
tagliatelle
baby corn
ginger
scallions
garlic
zucchini

1 Slice the carrot and zucchini diagonally into chunks. Slice the beans diagonally. Cut the baby corn diagonally in half.

2 Cook the pasta in plenty of boiling salted water according to the manufacturer's instructions, drain, then rinse under hot water. Toss in a little oil.

3 Heat 2 tbsp oil until smoking in a wok or skillet and add the ginger and garlic. Stir-fry for 30 seconds, then add the carrots, beans, and zucchini.

4 Stir-fry for 3–4 minutes, then stir in the yellow bean sauce. Stir-fry for 2 minutes, add the scallions, sherry, and pasta and stir-fry for 1 minute more until piping hot. Sprinkle with sesame seeds and serve immediately.

Spaghetti with Fresh Tomato Sauce

The heat from the pasta will release the delicious flavors of this sauce. Only use the really red and soft tomatoes – large ripe beefsteak tomatoes are ideal. Don't be tempted to use small hard tomatoes: they have very little flavor.

Serves 4

INGREDIENTS
4 large ripe tomatoes
2 garlic cloves, finely chopped
4 tbsp chopped fresh herbs such as
　basil, marjoram, oregano, or parsley
2/3 cup olive oil
salt and pepper
1 lb spaghetti

olive oil

garlic

spaghetti

tomato

2 Lift out with a perforated spoon and plunge into a bowl of cold water. Peel off the skins, then dry the tomatoes on paper towels.

3 Halve the tomatoes and squeeze out the seeds. Chop into 1/4 in cubes and mix with the garlic, herbs, olive oil, and seasoning in a non-metallic bowl. Cover and allow the flavors to mellow for at least 30 minutes.

1 Skin the tomatoes by placing in boiling water for 1 minute – no longer or they will become mushy.

4 Cook the pasta in plenty of boiling salted water.

5 Drain the pasta and mix with the sauce. Cover with a lid and leave for 2–3 minutes, toss again, and serve immediately.

VARIATION
Mix 3/4 cup pitted and chopped black Greek-style olives into the sauce just before serving.

Tagliatelle with Gorgonzola Sauce

Gorgonzola is a creamy Italian blue cheese. As an alternative you could use Danish Blue.

Serves 4

INGREDIENTS
2 tbsp butter, plus extra for tossing
   the pasta
½ lb Gorgonzola cheese
⅔ cup heavy or whipping cream
2 tbsp dry vermouth
1 tsp cornstarch
1 tbsp chopped fresh sage
salt and pepper
1 lb tagliatelle

tagliatelle

Gorgonzola cheese

sage

1 Melt 2 tbsp butter in a heavy saucepan (it needs to be thick-based to prevert the cheese from burning). Stir in 6 oz crumbled Gorgonzola cheese and stir over a very gentle heat for 2–3 minutes until the cheese is melted.

2 Pour in the cream, vermouth, and cornstarch, whisking well to amalgamate. Stir in the chopped sage, then taste and season. Cook, whisking all the time, until the sauce boils and thickens. Set aside.

3 Boil the pasta in plenty of salted water according to the manufacturer's instructions. Drain well and toss with a little butter.

4 Reheat the sauce gently, whisking well. Divide the pasta between 4 serving bowls, top with the sauce, and sprinkle over the remaining cheese. Serve immediately.

Pasta with Tomato and Cream Sauce

Here pasta is served with a deliciously rich version of ordinary tomato sauce.

Serves 4–6

INGREDIENTS
2 tbsp olive oil
2 garlic cloves, crushed
14 oz canned chopped tomatoes
⅔ cup heavy or whipping cream
2 tbsp chopped fresh herbs such as
    basil, oregano, or parsley
salt and pepper
4 cups pasta, any variety

olive oil

chopped tomatoes

parsley

pasta

garlic

1 Heat the oil in a medium saucepan, add the garlic, and cook for 2 minutes until golden.

COOK'S TIP
If you are really in a hurry, buy a good ready-made tomato sauce and simply stir in the cream and simmer until thickened.

2 Stir in the tomatoes, bring to a boil and simmer uncovered for 20 minutes, stirring occasionally to prevent sticking. The sauce is ready when you can see the oil separating on top.

3 Add the cream, bring slowly to a boil again, and simmer until slightly thickened. Stir in the herbs, taste, and season well.

4 Cook the pasta in plenty of boiling salted water according to the manufacturer's instructions. Drain well and toss with the sauce. Serve piping hot, sprinkled with extra herbs if liked.

Tagliatelle with Pea Sauce, Asparagus and Broad Beans

A creamy pea sauce makes a wonderful combination with the crunchy young vegetables.

Serves 4

INGREDIENTS
1 tbsp olive oil
1 garlic clove, crushed
6 scallions, sliced
1 cup fresh or frozen baby peas, defrosted
12 oz fresh young asparagus
2 tbsp chopped fresh sage, plus extra leaves, to garnish
finely grated rind of 2 lemons
1¾ cups fresh vegetable stock or water
8 oz fresh or frozen broad beans, defrosted
1 lb tagliatelle
4 tbsp low-fat yogurt

lemon
garlic
asparagus
broad beans
peas
yogurt
tagliatelle
sage
scallions

1 Heat the oil in a pan. Add the garlic and scallions and cook gently for 2–3 minutes until softened.

2 Add the peas and ⅓ of the asparagus, together with the sage, lemon rind and stock or water. Bring to a boil, reduce the heat and simmer for 10 minutes until tender. Purée in a blender until smooth.

3 Meanwhile remove the outer skins from the broad beans and discard.

4 Cut the remaining asparagus into 2 in lengths trimming off any tough fibrous stems, and blanch in boiling water for 2 minutes.

5 Cook the tagliatelle following the instructions on the side of the package until *al dente*. Drain well.

COOK'S TIP

Frozen peas and beans have been suggested here to cut down the preparation time, but the dish tastes even better if you use fresh young vegetables when in season.

6 Add the cooked asparagus and shelled beans to the sauce and reheat. Stir in the yogurt and toss into the tagliatelle. Garnish with a few extra sage leaves and serve.

Rigatoni with Garlic Crumbs

A hot and spicy dish – halve the quantity of chili if you like a milder flavor. The bacon is an addition for meat-eaters; leave it out or replace it with sliced mushrooms, if you prefer.

Serves 4–6

INGREDIENTS
3 tbsp olive oil
2 shallots, chopped
8 slices bacon, chopped (optional)
2 tsp crushed dried chilies
14 oz canned chopped tomatoes with garlic and herbs
6 slices white bread
½ cup butter
2 garlic cloves, chopped
1 lb rigatoni
salt and pepper

olive oil

garlic

rigatoni

shallots   *dried chilies*

1 Heat the oil in a medium saucepan and fry the shallots and bacon gently for 6–8 minutes until golden. Add the dried chilies and chopped tomatoes, half-cover, and simmer for 20 minutes.

2 Meanwhile cut the crusts off the bread and discard them. Reduce the bread to crumbs in a food processor.

3 Heat the butter in a skillet, add the garlic and bread crumbs and stir-fry until golden and crisp. (Don't let the crumbs catch and burn or the dish will be ruined!)

4 Cook the pasta in boiling salted water according to the manufacturer's instructions. Drain well.

5 Toss the pasta with the tomato sauce and divide between 4 serving bowls.

6 Sprinkle with the crumbs and serve immediately.

Tortellini with Cream, Butter and Cheese

This is an indulgent but quick alternative to macaroni and cheese. Meat-eaters could stir in some ham or pepperoni, though it's delicious as it is!

Serves 4–6

INGREDIENTS
4 cups fresh tortellini
salt and pepper
4 tbsp butter
1¼ cups heavy cream
¼ lb piece fresh Parmesan cheese
freshly grated nutmeg

1 Cook the pasta in plenty of boiling salted water according to the manufacturer's instructions.

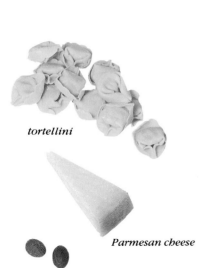

tortellini

Parmesan cheese

nutmeg

COOK'S TIP
Other hard grating cheeses can be used here, but don't try to use light cream or it will curdle.

2 Meanwhile melt the butter in a medium saucepan and stir in the cream. Bring to a boil and cook for 2–3 minutes until slightly thickened.

3 Grate the Parmesan cheese and stir ¾ cup into the sauce until melted. Season to taste with salt, pepper, and nutmeg. Preheat the broiler.

4 Drain the pasta well and spoon into a buttered heatproof serving dish. Pour over the sauce, sprinkle over the remaining cheese, and place under the broiler until brown and bubbling. Serve immediately.

Baked Tortellini with Three Cheeses

Serve this straight out of the oven while the cheese is still runny. If smoked mozzarella cheese is not available, try using a smoked German cheese or even grated smoked Cheddar.

Serves 4–6

INGREDIENTS
1 lb fresh tortellini
salt and pepper
2 eggs
1½ cups ricotta or cottage cheese
2 tbsp butter
1 oz fresh basil leaves
¼ lb smoked cheese, sliced
4 tbsp freshly grated Parmesan cheese

tortellini

smoked cheese

basil

eggs

1 Preheat the oven to 375°F. Cook the tortellini in plenty of boiling salted water according to the manufacturer's instructions. Drain well.

2 Beat the eggs with the ricotta cheese and season well with salt and pepper. Use the butter to grease an ovenproof dish. Spoon in half the tortellini, pour over half the ricotta mixture, and cover with half the basil leaves.

3 Cover with the smoked cheese and remaining basil. Top with the rest of the tortellini and spread over the remaining ricotta.

4 Sprinkle evenly with the Parmesan cheese. Bake in the oven for 35–45 minutes or until golden brown and bubbling. Serve immediately.

Pasta Shells with Tomatoes and Arugula

This pretty-colored pasta dish relies for its success on a salad green called arugula. Available in large supermarkets, it is a leaf easily grown in the garden or a window box and tastes slightly peppery.

Serves 4

INGREDIENTS
1 lb shell pasta
salt and pepper
1 lb very ripe cherry tomatoes
3 tbsp olive oil
3 oz fresh arugula
Parmesan cheese

olive oil

pasta shells

cherry tomatoes

arugula

Parmesan cheese

1 Cook the pasta in plenty of boiling salted water according to the manufacturer's instructions. Drain well.

2 Halve the tomatoes. Trim, wash, and dry the arugula.

3 Heat the oil in a large saucepan, add the tomatoes, and cook for barely 1 minute. The tomatoes should only just heat through and not disintegrate.

4 Shave the Parmesan cheese using a rotary vegetable peeler.

5 Add the pasta, then the arugula. Carefully stir to mix and heat through. Season well with salt and freshly ground black pepper. Serve immediately with plenty of shaved Parmesan cheese.

Pasta Tossed with Broiled Vegetables

A hearty dish to be eaten with crusty bread and washed down with a robust red wine. Try barbecuing the vegetables for a really smoky flavor.

Serves 4

INGREDIENTS
1 medium eggplant
2 medium zucchini
1 medium red bell pepper
8 garlic cloves, unpeeled
about ⅔ cup good olive oil
salt and pepper
1 lb ribbon pasta (pappardelle)
few sprigs fresh thyme, to garnish

olive oil

zucchini

eggplant

ribbon pasta

thyme

garlic

pepper

1 Preheat the broiler. Slice the eggplant and zucchini lengthwise.

2 Halve the bell pepper, cut out the stalk and white pith, and scrape out the seeds. Slice lengthwise into 8 pieces.

3 Line a broiler pan with foil and arrange the vegetables and unpeeled garlic in a single layer on top. Brush liberally with oil and season well with salt and pepper.

4 Grill until slightly charred, turning once. If necessary, cook the vegetables in 2 batches.

5 Cool the garlic, remove the charred skins, and halve. Toss the vegetables with olive oil and keep warm.

6 Meanwhile, cook the pasta in plenty of boiling salted water according to the manufacturer's instructions. Drain well and toss with the vegetables. Serve immediately, garnished with sprigs of thyme and accompanied by plenty of country bread.

Green Pasta with Avocado Sauce

This is an unusual sauce with a pale green color, studded with red tomato. It has a luxurious velvety texture. The sauce is rich, so you don't need much for a filling meal.

Serves 6

INGREDIENTS
3 ripe tomatoes
2 large ripe avocados
2 tbsp butter, plus extra for tossing
   the pasta
1 garlic clove, crushed
1½ cups heavy cream
salt and pepper
dash of Tabasco sauce
1 lb green tagliatelle
freshly grated Parmesan cheese
4 tbsp sour cream

tagliatelle

tomatoes

avocado

garlic

1 Halve the tomatoes and remove the cores. Squeeze out the seeds and cut the tomatoes into dice. Set aside.

2 Halve the avocados, take out the pits, and peel. Roughly chop the flesh.

3 Melt the butter in a saucepan and add the garlic. Cook for 1 minute, then add the cream and chopped avocados. Raise the heat, stirring constantly to break up the avocados.

4 Add the diced tomatoes and season to taste with salt, pepper, and a little Tabasco sauce. Keep warm.

5 Cook the pasta in plenty of boiling salted water according to the manufacturer's instructions. Drain well and toss with a knob of butter.

6 Divide the pasta between 4 warmed bowls and spoon over the sauce. Sprinkle with grated Parmesan and top with a spoonful of sour cream.

Spaghetti with Creamy Mussel and Saffron Sauce

In this recipe the pasta is tossed with a delicious pale yellow mussel sauce, streaked with yellow threads of saffron. Powdered saffron will do just as well, but don't use turmeric – the flavor will be too strong.

Serves 4

INGREDIENTS
2 lb live mussels
2/3 cup dry white wine
2 shallots, finely chopped
2 tbsp butter
2 garlic cloves, crushed
2 tsp cornstarch
1 1/4 cups heavy cream
pinch of saffron threads
salt and pepper
juice of 1/2 lemon
1 egg yolk
1 lb spaghetti
chopped fresh parsley, to garnish

spaghetti   *parsley*

mussels

garlic   *shallots*

1 Scrub the mussels and rinse well. Pull off any 'beards' and leave the shellfish to soak in cold water for 30 minutes. Tap each mussel sharply after this time. Any that do not close immediately are dead and should be thrown away.

2 Drain the mussels and place in a large saucepan. Add the wine and shallots, cover, and cook (shaking frequently) over a high heat for 5–10 minutes until the mussels are open. If some do not open at this stage, throw them out.

3 Pass through a strainer, reserving the liquid. Remove most of the mussels from their shells. Reserve some in the shell to use as a garnish. Boil the reserved liquid rapidly in a medium saucepan until reduced by half.

4 Melt the butter in another saucepan, add the garlic, and cook until golden. Stir in the cornstarch and gradually stir in the cooking liquid and the cream. Add the saffron and seasoning and simmer until slightly thickened.

5 Stir in lemon juice to taste, then the egg yolk and mussels. Keep warm, but do not boil.

6 Cook the pasta in plenty of boiling salted water according to the manufacturer's instructions. Drain well. Toss the mussels with the spaghetti, garnish with the reserved mussels in their shells, and sprinkle with the chopped parsley. Serve immediately with lots of crusty bread.

Pasta Spirals with Pepperoni and Tomato Sauce

A warming supper dish, perfect for cold winter nights. All types of sausage are suitable, but if using raw sausages, make sure that they go in with the onion to cook thoroughly.

Serves 4

INGREDIENTS
1 medium onion
1 red bell pepper
1 green bell pepper
2 tbsp olive oil, plus extra for tossing the pasta
1¾ lb canned chopped tomatoes
2 tbsp tomato paste
2 tsp paprika
6 oz pepperoni or chorizo (spicy sausage)
3 tbsp chopped fresh parsley
salt and pepper
1 lb pasta spirals (fusilli)

pasta spirals

pepperoni

bell peppers

onion

parsley

1 Chop the onion. Halve and seed the bell peppers, removing the cores, then cut the flesh into dice.

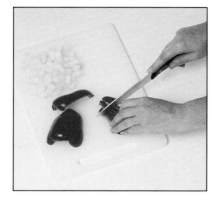

2 Heat the oil in a medium saucepan, add the onion, and cook for 2–3 minutes until beginning to color. Stir in the bell peppers, tomatoes, tomato paste, and paprika, bring to a boil and simmer, uncovered, for 15–20 minutes until reduced and thickened.

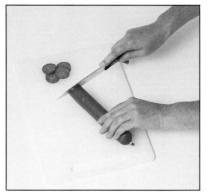

3 Slice the pepperoni and stir into the sauce with 2 tbsp chopped parsley. Season to taste.

4 While the sauce is simmering, cook the pasta in plenty of boiling salted water according to the manufacturer's instructions. Drain well. Toss the pasta with the remaining parsley and a little extra olive oil. Divide between warmed bowls and top with the sauce.

Spaghetti with Tomato and Clam Sauce

Small sweet clams make this a delicately succulent sauce. Mussels would make a good substitute, but don't be tempted to use seafood pickled in vinegar – the result will be inedible!

Serves 4

INGREDIENTS
2 lb live small clams, or 2 × 14 oz
   cans clams in brine, drained
6 tbsp olive oil
2 garlic cloves, crushed
1 lb 5 oz canned chopped tomatoes
3 tbsp chopped fresh parsley
salt and pepper
1 lb spaghetti

1 If using live clams, place them in a bowl of cold water and rinse several times to remove any grit or sand. Drain.

spaghetti

olive oil

parsley

garlic

clams

2 Heat the oil in a saucepan and add the clams. Stir over a high heat until the clams open. Throw away any that do not open. Transfer the clams to a bowl with a perforated spoon.

3 Reduce the clam juice left in the pan to almost nothing by boiling fast; this will also concentrate the flavor. Add the garlic and fry until golden. Pour in the tomatoes, bring to a boil, and cook for 3–4 minutes until reduced. Stir in the clam mixture or canned clams, and half the parsley and heat through. Season.

4 Cook the pasta in plenty of boiling salted water according to the manufacturer's instructions. Drain well and transfer to a warm serving dish. Pour over the sauce and sprinkle with the remaining parsley.

Pasta with Tuna, Capers, and Anchovies

This piquant sauce could be made without the addition of tomatoes – just heat the oil, add the other ingredients, and heat through gently before tossing with the pasta.

Serves 4

INGREDIENTS
14 oz canned tuna fish in oil
2 tbsp olive oil
2 garlic cloves, crushed
1¾ lb canned chopped tomatoes
6 canned anchovy fillets, drained
2 tbsp capers in vinegar, drained
2 tbsp chopped fresh basil
salt and pepper
1 lb rigatoni, garganelle or penne
fresh basil sprigs, to garnish

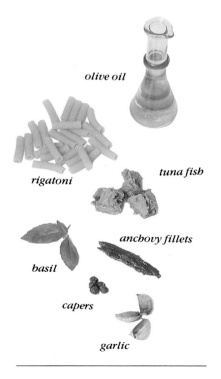

olive oil

rigatoni

tuna fish

anchovy fillets

basil

capers

garlic

1 Drain the oil from the tuna into a saucepan, add the olive oil, and heat gently until it stops 'spitting'.

2 Add the garlic and fry until golden. Stir in the tomatoes and simmer for 25 minutes until thickened.

3 Flake the tuna and cut the anchovies in half. Stir into the sauce with the capers and chopped basil. Season well.

4 Cook the pasta in plenty of boiling salted water according to the manufacturer's instructions. Drain well and toss with the sauce. Garnish with fresh basil sprigs.

Pasta Bows with Smoked Salmon and Dill

In Italy, pasta cooked with smoked salmon is becoming very fashionable. This is a quick and luxurious sauce.

Serves 4

INGREDIENTS
6 scallions, sliced
4 tbsp butter
6 tbsp dry white wine or vermouth
2 cups heavy cream
salt and pepper
freshly grated nutmeg
½ lb smoked salmon
2 tbsp chopped fresh dill or 1 tbsp dried dill
freshly squeezed lemon juice
1 lb pasta bows (farfalle)

pasta bows

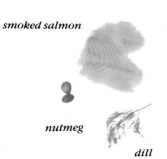

lemon

scallions

smoked salmon

nutmeg

dill

1 Slice the scallions finely. Melt the butter in a saucepan and fry the scallions for 1 minute until softened.

2 Add the wine and boil hard to reduce to about 2 tbsp. Stir in the cream and add salt, pepper, and nutmeg to taste. Bring to a boil and simmer for 2–3 minutes until slightly thickened.

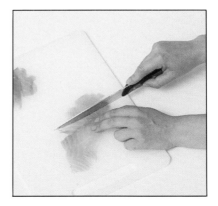

3 Cut the smoked salmon into 1 in squares and stir into the sauce with the dill. Taste and add a little lemon juice. Keep warm.

4 Cook the pasta in plenty of boiling salted water according to the manufacturer's instructions. Drain well. Toss the pasta with the sauce and serve immediately.

Shrimp with Tagliatelle and Pesto in Packets

A quick and impressive dish that is easy to prepare in advance and cook at the last minute. When the packets are opened, the filling smells wonderful.

Serves 4

INGREDIENTS
1½ lb medium raw shrimp, shells on
1 lb tagliatelle or similar pasta
salt and pepper
⅔ cup fresh pesto sauce or ready-
    made equivalent
4 tsp olive oil
1 garlic clove, crushed
8 tbsp dry white wine

tagliatelle

olive oil

shrimp

pesto sauce

garlic

1 Preheat the oven to 400°F. Twist the heads off the shrimp and discard.

2 Cook the tagliatelle in plenty of boiling salted water for 2 minutes only, then drain. Mix with half the pesto.

3 Cut 4 × 12 in squares of parchment paper and place 1 tsp olive oil in the center of each. Pile equal amounts of pasta in the middle of each square.

4 Top with equal amounts of shrimp and spoon the remaining pesto mixed with the crushed garlic over the shrimp. Season with black pepper and sprinkle each serving with 2 tbsp wine.

5 Brush the edges of the paper lightly with water and bring them loosely up around the filling, twisting tightly to enclose. (The parcels should look like money bags!)

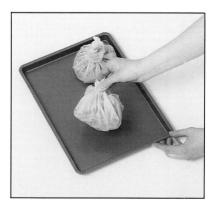

6 Place the parcels on a baking sheet. Bake in the oven for 10–15 minutes. Serve immediately, allowing each person to open their own packet.

Rigatoni with Spicy Sausage and Tomato Sauce

This is really a shortcut to Bolognese sauce, using the wonderful fresh spicy sausages sold at every Italian grocers.

Serves 4

INGREDIENTS
1 lb fresh spicy Italian sausage
2 tbsp olive oil
1 medium onion, chopped
2 cups tomato coulis (strained, crushed tomatoes)
⅔ cup dry red wine
6 sun-dried tomatoes in oil, drained
salt and pepper
1 lb rigatoni or similar pasta
freshly grated Parmesan cheese, to serve

rigatoni

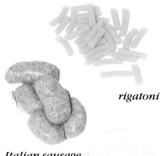
Italian sausage

Parmesan cheese

onion

sun-dried tomatoes

1 Squeeze the sausages out of their skins into a bowl and break up the meat.

2 Heat the oil in a medium saucepan and add the onion. Cook for 5 minutes until soft and golden. Stir in the sausage meat, browning it all over and breaking up the lumps with a wooden spoon. Pour in the coulis and the wine. Bring to a boil.

3 Slice the sun-dried tomatoes and add to the sauce. Simmer for 3 minutes until reduced, stirring occasionally. Season to taste.

4 Cook the pasta in plenty of boiling salted water according to the manufacturer's instructions. Drain well and top with the sauce. Serve with grated Parmesan cheese.

Pasta with Fresh Tomato and Smoky Bacon Sauce

A wonderful sauce to prepare in mid-summer when the tomatoes are ripe and sweet.

Serves 4

INGREDIENTS
2 lb ripe tomatoes
6 slices bacon
4 tbsp butter
1 medium onion, chopped
salt and pepper
1 tbsp chopped fresh oregano or 1 tsp
    dried oregano
1 lb pasta, any variety
freshly grated Parmesan cheese, to
    serve

pasta

oregano

tomatoes

onion

bacon

Parmesan cheese

1 Plunge the tomatoes into boiling water for 1 minute, then into cold water to stop them from becoming mushy. Slip off the skins. Halve the tomatoes, remove the seeds and cores, and roughly chop the flesh.

2 Remove the rind and roughly chop the bacon.

3 Melt the butter in a saucepan and add the bacon. Fry until lightly brown, then add the onion and cook gently for 5 minutes until softened. Add the tomatoes, salt, pepper, and oregano. Simmer gently for 10 minutes.

4 Cook the pasta in plenty of boiling salted water according to the manufacturer's instructions. Drain well and toss with the sauce. Serve with grated Parmesan cheese.

Pasta with Shrimp and Feta Cheese

This dish combines the richness of fresh shrimp with the tartness of feta cheese. Goat cheese could be used as an alternative.

Serves 4

INGREDIENTS
1 lb medium raw shrimp
6 scallions
4 tbsp butter
½ lb feta cheese
salt and pepper
small bunch fresh chives
1 lb penne, garganelle, or rigatoni

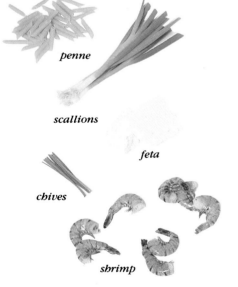

penne

scallions

feta

chives

shrimp

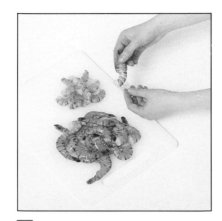

1 Remove the heads from the shrimp by twisting and pulling off. Peel the shrimp and discard the shells. Chop the scallions.

2 Melt the butter in a skillet and stir in the shrimp. When they turn pink, add the scallions and cook gently for 1 minute.

3 Cut the feta into ½ in cubes.

4 Stir the feta cheese into the shrimp mixture, and season with plenty of black pepper.

5 Cut the chives into 1 in lengths and stir half into the shrimp.

6 Cook the pasta in plenty of boiling salted water according to the manufacturer's instructions. Drain well, pile into a warmed serving dish, and top with the sauce. Scatter with the remaining chives and serve.

Tagliatelle with Prosciutto and Parmesan

A really simple dish, prepared in minutes from the best ingredients.

Serves 4

INGREDIENTS
¼ lb prosciutto
1 lb tagliatelle
salt and pepper
6 tbsp butter
½ cup freshly grated Parmesan
   cheese
few fresh sage leaves, to garnish

tagliatelle

sage

prosciutto

Parmesan cheese

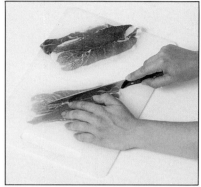

1 Cut the prosciutto into strips the same width as the tagliatelle. Cook the pasta in plenty of boiling salted water according to manufacturer's instructions.

2 Meanwhile, melt the butter gently in a saucepan, stir in the prosciutto strips and heat through, but do not fry.

3 Drain the tagliatelle well and pile into a warm serving dish.

4 Sprinkle over all the Parmesan cheese and pour over the buttery prosciutto. Season well with black pepper and garnish with the sage leaves.

Pasta with Spinach and Anchovy Sauce

Deliciously earthy, this would make a good entree or light supper dish. Add golden raisins for something really special.

Serves 4

INGREDIENTS
2 lb fresh spinach or 1¼ lb frozen leaf
    spinach, thawed
1 lb angel hair pasta
salt
4 tbsp olive oil
3 tbsp pine nuts
2 garlic cloves, crushed
6 canned anchovy fillets or whole
    salted anchovies, drained and
    chopped
butter, for tossing the pasta

olive oil

pine nuts

spinach

anchovy fillets

garlic   *angel hair pasta*

1 Wash the spinach well and remove the tough stalks. Drain thoroughly. Place in a large saucepan with only the water that still clings to the leaves. Cover with a lid and cook over a high heat, shaking the pan occasionally, until the spinach is just wilted and still bright green. Drain.

2 Cook the pasta in plenty of boiling salted water according to the manufacturer's instructions.

3 Heat the oil in a saucepan and fry the pine nuts until golden. Remove with a perforated spoon. Add the garlic to the oil in the pan and fry until golden. Add the anchovies.

4 Stir in the spinach, and cook for 2–3 minutes or until heated through. Stir in the pine nuts. Drain the pasta, toss in a little butter, and transfer to a warmed serving bowl. Top with the sauce and fork through roughly.

Lasagne al Forno

The classic version of this dish is pasta layered with meat sauce and creamy béchamel sauce. You could vary it by using mozzarella cheese instead of the béchamel sauce, or by mixing ricotta cheese, Parmesan, and herbs together instead of the traditional meat sauce.

Serves 4–6

INGREDIENTS
about 12 sheets dried lasagne
1 recipe Bolognese Sauce
about ½ cup freshly grated Parmesan
   cheese
tomato slices and parsley sprig, to
   garnish

BÉCHAMEL SAUCE
3¾ cups milk
sliced onion, carrot, celery
few whole peppercorns
½ cup butter
⅔ cup all-purpose flour
salt and pepper
freshly grated nutmeg

1 First make the béchamel sauce. Pour the milk into a saucepan and add the vegetables and peppercorns. Bring to boiling point, remove from the heat, and leave to infuse for at least 30 minutes.

2 Strain the milk into a pitcher. Melt the butter in the same saucepan and stir in the flour. Cook, stirring, for 2 minutes.

3 Remove from the heat and add the milk all at once, whisk well, and return to the heat. Bring to a boil, whisking all the time, then simmer for 2–3 minutes, stirring constantly until thickened. Season to taste with salt, pepper, and nutmeg.

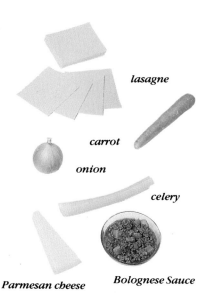

lasagne

carrot

onion

celery

Parmesan cheese   *Bolognese Sauce*

4 Preheat the oven to 350°F. If necessary, cook the sheets of lasagne in plenty of boiling salted water according to the instructions. Lift out with a perforated spoon and drain on a clean dish towel. Spoon one-third of the meat sauce into a buttered baking dish.

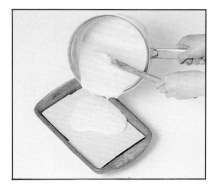

5 Cover the meat sauce with 4 sheets of lasagne and spread with one-third of the béchamel sauce. Repeat twice more, finishing with a layer of béchamel sauce covering the whole top.

6 Sprinkle with Parmesan cheese and bake in the oven for about 45 minutes until brown. Serve garnished with tomato slices and a sprig of parsley.

Cannelloni al Forno

A lighter alternative to the usual beef-filled, béchamel-coated version. Fill with ricotta, onion, and mushroom for a vegetarian recipe.

Serves 4–6

INGREDIENTS
4 cups boneless, skinned chicken
   breast, cooked
½ lb mushrooms
2 garlic cloves, crushed
2 tbsp chopped fresh parsley
1 tbsp chopped fresh tarragon
1 egg, beaten
salt and pepper
fresh lemon juice
12–18 cannelloni tubes
1 recipe Napoletana Sauce
½ cup freshly grated Parmesan
   cheese
1 sprig fresh parsley, to garnish

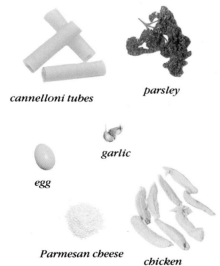

cannelloni tubes   *parsley*

garlic

egg

Parmesan cheese   *chicken*

1 Preheat the oven to 400°F. Place the chicken in a food processor and blend until finely ground. Transfer to a bowl.

2 Place the mushrooms, garlic, parsley, and tarragon in the food processor and blend until finely minced.

3 Beat the mushroom mixture into the chicken with the egg, salt and pepper, and lemon juice to taste.

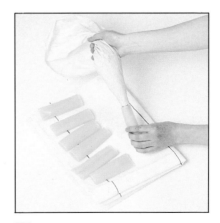

4 If necessary, cook the cannelloni in plenty of salted boiling water according to the manufacturer's instructions. Drain well on a clean dish towel.

5 Place the filling in a pastry bag fitted with a large plain tip. Use this to fill each tube of cannelloni.

6 Lay the filled cannelloni tightly together in a single layer in a buttered shallow ovenproof dish. Spoon over the tomato sauce and sprinkle with Parmesan cheese. Bake in the oven for 30 minutes, or until brown and bubbling. Serve garnished with a sprig of parsley.

Spaghetti alla Carbonara

It has been said that this dish was originally cooked by Italian coal miners, or charcoal-burners, hence the name 'carbonara'. The secret of its creamy sauce is not to overcook the egg.

Serves 4

INGREDIENTS
6 oz bacon
1 garlic clove, chopped
3 eggs
1 lb spaghetti
salt and pepper
4 tbsp freshly grated Parmesan cheese

bacon

garlic

eggs

spaghetti

Parmesan cheese

1 Cut the bacon into a dice and place in a medium saucepan. Place over the heat and fry in its own fat with the garlic until brown. Keep warm until needed.

2 Whisk the eggs together in a bowl.

3 Cook the spaghetti in plenty of boiling salted water according to the manufacturer's instructions until *al dente*. Drain well.

4 Quickly transfer the spaghetti to the pan with the bacon and stir in the eggs, a little salt, lots of pepper, and half the cheese. Toss well to mix. The eggs should half-cook with the heat from the spaghetti. Serve in warm bowls with the remaining cheese.

Pasta with Bolognese Sauce

Traditional Bolognese sauce contains chicken livers to add richness, but you can leave them out and replace with an equal quantity of ground beef.

Serves 4–6

INGREDIENTS

3 oz pancetta or bacon in a piece
4 oz chicken livers
4 tbsp butter, plus extra for tossing the pasta
1 medium onion, finely chopped
1 medium carrot, diced
1 celery stick, finely chopped
½ lb lean ground beef
2 tbsp tomato paste
½ cup dry white wine
1 cup beef stock or water
salt and pepper
freshly grated nutmeg
1 lb tagliatelle, spaghetti, or fettuccine
freshly grated Parmesan cheese, to serve

tagliatelle

carrot

chicken livers

onion

celery

bacon

ground beef

COOK'S TIP

If you like a richer sauce, stir in ⅔ cup heavy cream or milk when the sauce has finished cooking.

1 Cut the pancetta into a dice. Trim the chicken livers, removing any fat or gristle and any 'green' bits, which will be bitter if left on. Roughly chop the livers.

2 Melt 4 tbsp butter in a saucepan and add the bacon. Cook for 2–3 minutes until beginning to brown. Add the onion, carrot, and celery and brown these too.

3 Stir in the ground beef and brown over a high heat, breaking it up with a spoon. Stir in the chicken livers and cook for 2–3 minutes. Add the tomato paste, mix well, and pour in the wine and stock. Season well with salt, pepper, and nutmeg. Bring to a boil, cover, and simmer gently for about 35 minutes, stirring occasionally.

4 Cook the pasta in plenty of boiling salted water according to the manufacturer's instructions. Drain well and toss with the extra butter. Toss the meat sauce with the pasta and serve with plenty of Parmesan cheese.

Fettuccine all'Alfredo

A classic dish from Rome, Fettuccine all'Alfredo is simply pasta tossed with heavy cream, butter, and freshly grated Parmesan cheese. Popular less classic additions are peas and strips of ham.

Serves 4

INGREDIENTS
2 tbsp butter
⅔ cup heavy cream, plus 4 tbsp extra
1 lb fettuccine
freshly grated nutmeg
½ cup freshly grated Parmesan
   cheese, plus extra to serve
salt and pepper

fettuccine

nutmeg

Parmesan cheese

1 Place the butter and ⅔ cup cream in a heavy saucepan, bring to a boil, and simmer for 1 minute until slightly thickened.

2 Cook the fettuccine in plenty of boiling salted water according to the manufacturer's instructions, but for 2 minutes less time. The pasta should still be a little firm.

3 Drain very well and transfer to the pan with the cream sauce.

4 Place on the heat and toss the pasta in the sauce to coat.

5 Add the extra 4 tbsp cream, the cheese, salt and pepper to taste, and a little grated nutmeg. Toss until well coated and heated through. Serve immediately with extra grated Parmesan cheese.

Spaghetti Olio e Aglio

This is another classic recipe from Rome. A quick and filling dish, originally the food of the poor involving nothing more than pasta, garlic, and olive oil, but now fast becoming fashionable.

Serves 4

INGREDIENTS
2 garlic cloves
2 tbsp fresh parsley
½ cup olive oil
1 lb spaghetti
salt and pepper

spaghetti

olive oil

parsley

garlic

1 Finely chop the garlic.

2 Chop the parsley roughly.

3 Heat the olive oil in a medium saucepan and add the garlic and a pinch of salt. Cook gently, stirring all the time, until golden. If the garlic becomes too brown, it will taste bitter.

4 Meanwhile cook the spaghetti in plenty of boiling salted water according to the manufacturer's instructions. Drain well.

5 Toss with the warm – not sizzling – garlic and oil and add plenty of black pepper and the parsley. Serve immediately.

Paglia e Fieno

The title of this dish translates as 'straw and hay', which refers to the yellow and green colors of the pasta when mixed together. Using fresh peas makes all the difference to this dish.

Serves 4

INGREDIENTS
4 tbsp butter
2 cups frozen petits pois (small peas)
   or 2 lb fresh peas, shelled
⅔ cup heavy cream, plus 4 tbsp extra
1 lb tagliatelle (plain and spinach,
   mixed)
½ cup freshly grated Parmesan
   cheese, plus extra to serve
salt and pepper
freshly grated nutmeg

tagliatelle

peas

Parmesan cheese

COOK'S TIP
Sautéed mushrooms and narrow strips of cooked ham also make a good addition.

1 Melt the butter in a heavy saucepan and add the peas. Sauté for 2–3 minutes, then add the cream, bring to a boil, and simmer for 1 minute until slightly thickened.

2 Cook the fettuccine in plenty of boiling salted water according to the manufacturer's instructions, but for 2 minutes' less time. The pasta should still be *al dente*. Drain very well and transfer to the pan with the cream and pea sauce.

3 Place on the heat and toss the pasta in the sauce to coat. Pour in the extra cream, the cheese, salt and pepper to taste, and a little grated nutmeg. Toss until well coated and heated through. Serve immediately with extra Parmesan cheese.

Pasta Napoletana

The simple classic cooked tomato sauce with no adornments!

Serves 4

INGREDIENTS

2 lb fresh ripe red tomatoes or 1¾ lb
  canned plum tomatoes with juice
1 medium onion, chopped
1 medium carrot, diced
1 celery stick, diced
⅔ cup dry white wine (optional)
1 sprig fresh parsley
salt and pepper
pinch of superfine sugar
1 tbsp chopped fresh oregano or 1 tsp
  dried oregano
1 lb pasta, any variety
freshly grated Parmesan cheese, to
  serve

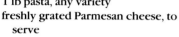

pasta

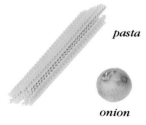

onion

tomatoes

celery

parsley

carrot

Parmesan cheese

1 Roughly chop the tomatoes and place in a medium saucepan.

2 Put all the ingredients – except the oregano, pasta, and cheese – into the pan with the tomatoes. Bring to a boil and simmer, half-covered, for 45 minutes until very thick, stirring occasionally. Pass through a strainer or liquidize and strain to remove the tomato seeds, then stir in the oregano. Taste to check the seasoning and adjust if necessary.

3 Cook the pasta in plenty of boiling salted water according to the manufacturer's instructions. Drain well.

4 Toss the pasta with the sauce. Serve with grated Parmesan cheese.

Pasta with Pesto Sauce

Don't skimp on the fresh basil – this is the most wonderful sauce in the world! This pesto can also be used as a basting sauce for broiled chicken or fish, or rubbed over a leg of lamb before baking.

Serves 4

INGREDIENTS
2 garlic cloves
salt and pepper
½ cup pine nuts
1 cup fresh basil leaves
⅔ cup olive oil (not extra-virgin as it
　is too strong)
4 tbsp unsalted butter, softened
4 tbsp freshly grated Parmesan cheese
1 lb spaghetti

olive oil

spaghetti

pine nuts

Parmesan cheese

basil

1 Peel the garlic and process in a food processor with a little salt and the pine nuts until broken up. Add the basil leaves and continue mixing to a paste.

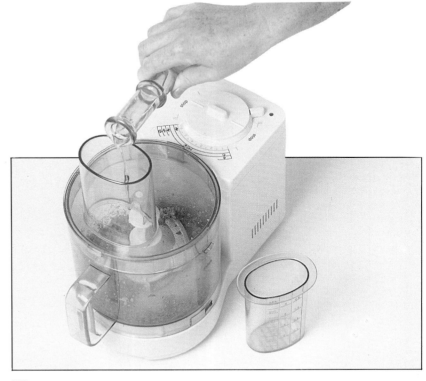

2 Gradually add the olive oil, little by little, until the mixture is creamy and thick.

3 Mix in the butter and season with pepper. Mix in the cheese. (Alternatively, you can make the pesto by hand using a pestle and mortar.)

4 Store the pesto in a jar (with a layer of olive oil on top to exclude the air) in the fridge until needed.

5 Cook the pasta in plenty of boiling salted water according to the manufacturer's instructions. Drain well.

COOK'S TIP

A good pesto can be made using parsley instead of basil and walnuts instead of pine nuts. To make it go further, add a spoonful or two of fromage frais. 'Red' pesto includes sun-dried tomato paste and pounded roasted red peppers.

6 Toss the pasta with half the pesto and serve in warm bowls with the remaining pesto spooned on top.

Rotolo di Pasta

A giant jelly roll of pasta with a spinach filling, that is poached, sliced, and baked with béchamel or tomato sauce. Use fresh homemade pasta for this recipe, or ask your local Italian grocer to make a large sheet of pasta for you.

Serves 6

INGREDIENTS
1½ lb frozen chopped spinach, thawed
4 tbsp butter
1 medium onion, chopped
4 oz ham or bacon, diced
½ lb ricotta or cottage cheese
1 egg
salt and pepper
freshly grated nutmeg
fresh spinach pasta made with 2 eggs and 1¾ cups flour
5½ cups Béchamel Sauce, warmed
½ cup freshly grated Parmesan cheese

onion

ricotta cheese

spinach

nutmeg

ham

1 Squeeze the excess moisture from the spinach and set aside.

2 Melt the butter in a saucepan and fry the onion until golden. Add the ham and fry until beginning to brown. Take off the heat and stir in the spinach. Cool slightly, then beat in the ricotta and egg. Season well with salt, pepper, and nutmeg.

3 Roll the pasta out to a rectangle about 12 × 16 in. Spread the filling all over, leaving a ½ in border all around the edge.

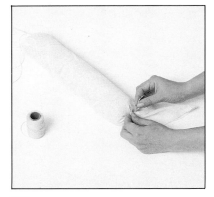

4 Roll up from the shorter end and wrap in cheesecloth to form a 'sausage', tying the ends securely with string. Poach in a very large pan (or fish poacher) of simmering water for 20 minutes or until firm. Carefully remove, drain, and unwrap. Cool.

5 When you are ready to finish the dish, preheat the oven to 400°F. Cut the pasta roll into 1 in slices. Spoon a little béchamel sauce over the base of a shallow baking dish and arrange the slices slightly overlapping each other.

6 Spoon over the remaining sauce, sprinkle with the cheese, and bake in the oven for 15–20 minutes or until browned and bubbling. Allow to stand for a few minutes before serving.

Pasta, Melon and Shrimp Salad

Orange-fleshed cantaloupe or Charentais melon looks spectacular in this salad. You could also use a mixture of honeydew, cantaloupe and watermelon.

Serves 4–6

INGREDIENTS
1½ cups pasta shapes
½ lb frozen shrimp, thawed and drained
1 large or 2 small melons
4 tbsp olive oil
1 tbsp tarragon vinegar
2 tbsp chopped fresh chives or parsley
sprigs of herbs, to garnish
Napa cabbage, to serve

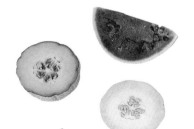

melons

pasta shapes

shrimp

Napa cabbage

1 Cook the pasta in boiling salted water according to the manufacturer's instructions. Drain well and allow to cool.

2 Peel the shrimp and discard the shells.

3 Halve the melon and remove the seeds with a teaspoon. Carefully scoop the flesh into balls with a melon baller and mix with the shrimp and pasta.

4 Whisk the oil, vinegar, and chopped herbs together. Pour on to the shrimp mixture and toss to coat. Cover and chill for at least 30 minutes.

5 Meanwhile shred the Napa cabbage and use to line a shallow bowl or the empty melon halves.

6 Pile the shrimp mixture onto the Napa cabbage and garnish with herbs.

Warm Pasta Salad with Ham, Egg, and Asparagus

In the summer months when the weather is hot, try serving your pasta *calda*, as a warm salad. Here it is served with ham, eggs, and asparagus. A mustard dressing made from the thick part of asparagus provides a rich accompaniment.

Serves 4

INGREDIENTS
1 lb asparagus
salt
1 lb dried tagliatelle
½ lb sliced cooked ham,
   ¼ in thick, cut into fingers
2 eggs, hard-cooked and sliced
2 oz Parmesan cheese, shaved

DRESSING
2 oz cooked potato
5 tbsp olive oil, preferably Sicilian
1 tbsp lemon juice
2 tsp Dijon mustard
½ cup vegetable stock

asparagus

tagliatelle

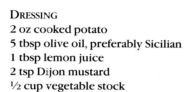

eggs

Parmesan cheese

ham

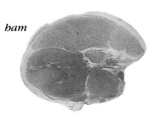

1 Bring a saucepan of salted water to the boil. Trim and discard the tough woody part of the asparagus. Cut the asparagus in half and boil the thicker halves for 12 minutes. After 6 minutes throw in the tips. Refresh under cold water until warm, then drain.

2 Finely chop 5 oz of the asparagus middle section. Place in a food processor with the dressing ingredients and process until smooth. Season to taste.

3 Boil the pasta in a large saucepan of salted water according to the packet instructions. Refresh under cold water until warm, and drain. Dress with the asparagus sauce and transfer to 4 pasta plates. Top with the ham, hard-cooked eggs, and asparagus tips. Finish with Parmesan cheese.

Chicken and Pasta Salad

This is a delicious way to use up left-over cooked chicken, and makes a filling meal.

Serves 4

INGREDIENTS
8 oz tri-colored pasta twists
2 tbsp bottled pesto sauce
1 tbsp olive oil
1 beefsteak tomato
12 pitted black olives
8 oz cooked green beans
12 oz cooked chicken, cubed
salt and freshly ground black pepper
fresh basil, to garnish

tomato

green beans

pesto sauce

basil

olive oil

pasta twists

chicken

black olives

1 Cook the pasta in plenty of boiling, salted water until *al dente* (for about 12 minutes or as directed on the package).

2 Drain the pasta and rinse in plenty of cold running water. Put into a bowl and stir in the pesto sauce and olive oil.

3 Skin the tomato by placing in boiling water for about 10 seconds and then into cold water, to loosen the skin.

4 Cut the tomato into small cubes and add to the pasta with the black olives, seasoning and green beans cut into 1 ½ in lengths. Add the cubed chicken. Toss gently together and transfer to a serving platter. Garnish with fresh basil.

Avocado, Tomato, and Mozzarella Pasta Salad with Pine Nuts

A salad made from ingredients representing the colors of the Italian flag – a sunny cheerful dish!

Serves 4

INGREDIENTS
1½ cups pasta bows (farfalle)
6 ripe red tomatoes
½ lb mozzarella cheese
1 large ripe avocado
2 tbsp pine nuts, toasted
1 sprig fresh basil, to garnish

DRESSING
6 tbsp olive oil
2 tbsp wine vinegar
1 tsp balsamic vinegar (optional)
1 tsp whole-grain mustard
pinch of sugar
salt and pepper
2 tbsp chopped fresh basil

olive oil

avocado

tomatoes

mozzarella cheese

basil

pine nuts   *pasta bows*

1 Cook the pasta in plenty of boiling salted water according to the manufacturer's instructions. Drain well and cool.

2 Slice the tomatoes and mozzarella cheese into thin rounds.

3 Halve the avocado, remove the pit, and peel off the skin. Slice the flesh lengthwise.

4 Whisk all the dressing ingredients together in a small bowl.

5 Arrange the tomato, mozzarella, and avocado in overlapping slices around the edge of a flat plate.

6 Toss the pasta with half the dressing and the chopped basil. Pile into the center of the plate. Pour over the remaining dressing, scatter over the pine nuts, and garnish with a sprig of fresh basil. Serve immediately.

Whole-wheat Pasta, Asparagus, and Potato Salad with Parmesan

A meal in itself, this is a real treat when made with fresh asparagus just in season.

Serves 4

INGREDIENTS
½ lb whole-wheat pasta shapes
4 tbsp extra-virgin olive oil
salt and pepper
12 oz baby new potatoes
½ lb fresh asparagus
¼ lb piece fresh Parmesan cheese

olive oil

asparagus

Parmesan cheese

pasta shapes

new potatoes

1 Cook the pasta in boiling salted water according to the manufacturer's instructions. Drain well and toss with the olive oil, salt, and pepper while still warm.

2 Wash the potatoes and cook in boiling salted water for 12–15 minutes or until tender. Drain and toss with the pasta.

3 Trim any woody ends off the asparagus and halve the stalks if very long. Blanch in boiling salted water for 6 minutes until bright green and still crunchy. Drain. Plunge into cold water to stop them cooking and allow to cool. Drain and dry on paper towels.

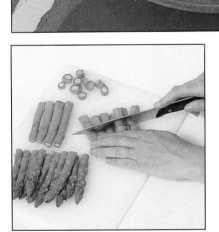

4 Toss the asparagus with the potatoes and pasta, season, and transfer to a shallow bowl. Using a rotary vegetable peeler, shave the Parmesan cheese over the salad.

Roquefort and Walnut Pasta Salad

This is a simple earthy salad, relying totally on the quality of the ingredients. There is no real substitute for the Roquefort – a blue-veined ewe's-milk cheese from southwestern France.

Serves 4

INGREDIENTS
½ lb pasta shapes
selection of salad leaves (such as arugula, frisée, lamb's lettuce, baby spinach, radicchio, etc.)
2 tbsp walnut oil
4 tbsp sunflower oil
2 tbsp red-wine vinegar or sherry vinegar
salt and pepper
½ lb Roquefort cheese, roughly crumbled
1 cup walnut halves

pasta shapes

Roquefort cheese   *walnuts*

salad leaves

COOK'S TIP
Try toasting the walnuts under the broiler for a couple of minutes to release the flavor.

1 Cook the pasta in plenty of boiling salted water according to the manufacturer's instructions. Drain well and cool. Wash and dry the salad leaves and place in a bowl.

2 Whisk together the walnut oil, sunflower oil, vinegar, and salt and pepper to taste.

3 Pile the pasta in the center of the leaves, scatter over the crumbled Roquefort, and pour over the dressing.

4 Scatter over the walnuts. Toss just before serving.

Mediterranean Salad with Basil

A type of Salade Niçoise with pasta, conjuring up all the sunny flavors of the Mediterranean.

Serves 4

INGREDIENTS
½ lb chunky pasta shapes
6 oz fine green beans
2 large ripe tomatoes
2 oz fresh basil leaves
7 oz can tuna fish in oil, drained
2 hard-cooked eggs, shelled and sliced
    or quartered
2 oz can anchovies, drained
capers and black olives

DRESSING
6 tbsp extra-virgin olive-oil
2 tbsp white-wine vinegar or lemon
    juice
2 garlic cloves, crushed
½ tsp Dijon mustard
2 tbsp chopped fresh basil
salt and pepper

olive oil

tomatoes

garlic

basil

pasta

anchovies

egg

green beans

tuna fish

1 Whisk all the ingredients for the dressing together and leave to infuse while you make the salad.

2 Cook the pasta in plenty of boiling salted water according to the manufacturer's instructions. Drain well and cool.

3 Trim the beans and blanch in boiling salted water for 3 minutes. Drain and refresh in cold water.

4 Slice or quarter the tomatoes and arrange on the bottom of a bowl. Toss with a little dressing and cover with a quarter of the basil leaves. Then cover with the beans. Toss with a little more dressing and cover with a third of the remaining basil.

5 Cover with the pasta tossed in a little more dressing, half the remaining basil and the roughly flaked tuna.

6 Arrange the eggs on top, then finally scatter over the anchovies, capers and black olives. Pour over the remaining dressing and garnish with the remaining basil. Serve immediately. Don't be tempted to chill this salad — all the flavor will be dulled.

Dark Chocolate Ravioli with White Chocolate and Cream Cheese Filling

This is a spectacular, chocolatey pasta, with cocoa powder added to the flour. The pasta packets contain a rich creamy-white filling.

Serves 4

INGREDIENTS
1½ cups all-purpose flour
¼ cup cocoa powder
2 tbsp confectioners' sugar
2 large eggs
salt
light cream and grated chocolate, to
    serve

FILLING
6 oz white chocolate
3 cups cream cheese
1 egg, plus 1 beaten egg to seal

eggs

cream cheese

white chocolate

cocoa powder

1 Make the pasta following the instructions for Basic Pasta Dough, but sifting the flour with the cocoa and confectioners' sugar before adding the eggs. Cover and rest for 30 minutes.

2 For the filling, break up the white chocolate and melt it in a bowl standing in a pan of barely simmering water. Cool slightly, then beat into the cream cheese with the egg. Spoon into a pastry bag fitted with a plain tip.

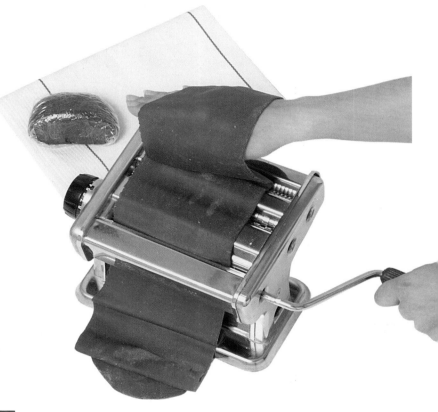

3 Cut the dough in half and wrap one portion in clear film (plastic wrap). Roll the pasta out thinly to a rectangle on a lightly floured surface, or use a pasta machine. Cover with a clean damp tea (dish) towel and repeat with the remaining pasta.

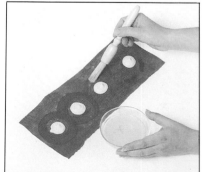

4 Pipe small mounds (about 1 tsp) of filling in even rows, spacing them at 1½ in intervals, across one piece of the dough. Using a pastry brush, brush the spaces of dough between the mounds with some beaten egg.

5 Using a rolling pin, lift the remaining sheet of pasta over the dough with the filling. Press down firmly between the pockets of filling, pushing out any trapped air. Cut into rounds with a serrated ravioli cutter or sharp knife. Transfer to a floured dish towel. Rest for 1 hour.

6 Bring a large pan of salted water to a boil and add the ravioli a few at a time, stirring to prevent them sticking together. Simmer gently for 3–5 minutes, remove with a perforated spoon. Serve with a generous splash of light cream and some grated chocolate.

Crisp Vermicelli Cakes with Honey and Walnuts

In this recipe the pasta is double-cooked for crispness, then soaked in honey and nuts to give a Middle Eastern flavor.

Serves 4

INGREDIENTS
½ lb vermicelli or angel hair pasta
salt
½ cup butter
1 ½ cups mixed nuts, such as walnuts
    and pistachios
½ cup granulated sugar
⅓ cup clear honey
2 tsp lemon juice

vermicelli

nuts

lemon

butter

honey

1 Preheat the oven to 350°F. Cook the pasta in plenty of boiling salted water according to the manufacturer's instructions. Drain well, return to the pan with the butter, and toss in the residual heat to coat. Cool.

2 Set 4 poaching rings on baking sheets. Divide the pasta into 8 mounds, then lightly press a mound of pasta evenly into each ring.

3 Chop the nuts and sprinkle half over the pasta. Top each ring with a mound of the remaining pasta and press down well. Bake in the oven for 40–45 minutes or until golden brown.

4 Meanwhile, place the sugar, honey, and ⅔ cup water in a medium saucepan and slowly bring to a boil, making sure that all the sugar is dissolved before it boils. Simmer for 10 minutes, add the lemon juice, and simmer for 5 minutes more. Set aside.

5 Carefully remove the baked pasta from the rings and place in an even layer on a shallow dish.

6 Pour over the syrup and scatter with the remaining nuts. Cool completely before serving.

Cinnamon Tagliatelle with Creamy Custard Sauce

The secret of this pudding is to roll the pasta out very thinly, giving delicious ribbons coated in a delicate vanilla sauce.

Serves 4

INGREDIENTS
1½ cups all-purpose flour
pinch of salt
2 tbsp confectioners' sugar
2 tsp ground cinnamon, plus extra for dusting the pasta
2 large eggs
melted butter, for tossing the pasta

CUSTARD
1 vanilla bean
2½ cups milk
6 egg yolks
¼–⅓ cup superfine sugar

butter

eggs

cinnamon

vanilla bean

1 Make the pasta following the instructions for Basic Pasta Dough, but sifting the flour with the confectioners' sugar and cinnamon before adding the eggs. Roll out thinly and cut into tagliatelle. Spread out on a clean, lightly floured dish towel to dry.

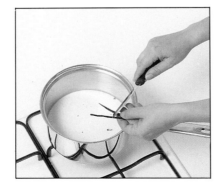

2 For the custard, split the vanilla bean and scrape out the seeds into a saucepan. Add the pod itself to the pan with the milk and slowly bring to a boil. Take the pan off the heat and allow to infuse for 10 minutes, then strain to remove the vanilla bean and seeds.

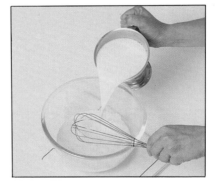

3 Whisk the egg yolks and sugar together in a medium bowl until pale and creamy. Slowly stir in the strained milk, return the pan to a low heat, and cook, stirring, until slightly thickened. Do not boil or the custard will curdle. Strain and keep warm.

4 Drop the tagliatelle into plenty of boiling salted water and cook until the water returns to the boil or until *al dente*. The pasta should have no hard core, and should be very pliable. Strain and toss with a little butter. Serve in warm bowls with the custard poured over. Dust with extra cinnamon if liked.

Tiramisu Surprise

The small pasta shapes incorporated into this dessert make a very pretty dish served in tall glasses.

Serves 4

INGREDIENTS

¼ lb small pasta shapes
salt
16 small ratafias, macaroons, or
    Amaretti cookies
6 tbsp very strong black coffee
2 tbsp brandy
4 tbsp dark rum
1¾ cups mascarpone or other cream
    cheese
½ cup confectioners' sugar, sifted
⅔ cup whipping cream
3 oz chocolate shavings, to decorate

dark rum

pasta shapes

brandy   *chocolate*

ratafias

I Cook the pasta in plenty of boiling salted water according to the manufacturer's instructions. Drain well and cool.

2 Place the ratafias in 4 individual glasses and spoon over a layer of pasta. Mix together the coffee, brandy, and 2 tbsp of the rum, and pour this over the pasta layer.

3 Beat the mascarpone with the sugar and remaining rum until smooth. Stir in the cream and spoon the mixture equally between the glasses.

4 Sprinkle the chocolate shavings thickly on top of the cheese mixture to decorate and refrigerate for at least 1 hour before serving.

Pasta Timbales with Apricot Sauce

Orzo, or rice-shaped, pasta inspired this dessert made like a rice pudding, but with a difference! Other small soup pastas can be used if orzo cannot be found.

Serves 4

INGREDIENTS

¼ lb orzo or other soup pasta
⅓ cup superfine sugar
salt
2 tbsp butter
1 vanilla bean, split
3⅔ cups milk
1¼ cups ready-made vanilla pudding
3 tbsp kirsch
1 tbsp powdered gelatin
oil, for greasing
14 oz canned apricots in juice
lemon juice
fresh flowers, to decorate (optional)

custard

butter

pasta

apricots

lemon

1 Place the pasta, sugar, a pinch of salt, the butter, vanilla bean, and milk into a heavy saucepan and bring to a boil. Turn down the heat and simmer for 25 minutes until the pasta is tender and most of the liquid is absorbed. Stir frequently to prevent it from sticking.

2 Remove the vanilla bean and transfer the pasta to a bowl to cool. Stir in the custard and 2 tbsp of the kirsch.

3 Sprinkle the gelatin over 3 tbsp water in a small bowl set in a pan of barely simmering water. Allow to become spongy and heat gently to dissolve. Stir into the pasta.

4 Lightly oil 4 timbale molds and spoon in the pasta. Refrigerate for about 2 hours until set.

5 Meanwhile, liquidize the apricots, pass through a strainer, and add lemon juice and kirsch to taste. Dilute with a little water if too thick.

6 Loosen the pasta timbales from their molds and turn out onto individual plates. Spoon some apricot sauce around and serve, decorated with a few fresh flowers if liked.

Strawberry Conchiglie Salad with Kirsch and Raspberry Sauce

A divinely decadent dessert laced with liqueur and luscious raspberry sauce.

Serves 4

INGREDIENTS
6 oz pasta shells (conchiglie)
salt
½ lb fresh or frozen raspberries, thawed if frozen
1–2 tbsp superfine sugar
lemon juice
1 lb small fresh strawberries
flaked almonds
3 tbsp kirsch

pasta shells

raspberries

strawberries

almonds

1 Cook the pasta in plenty of boiling salted water according to the manufacturer's instructions. Drain well and cool.

2 Purée the raspberries in a food processor and pass through a strainer to remove the seeds.

3 Put the purée in a small saucepan with the sugar and simmer for 5–6 minutes, stirring occasionally. Add lemon juice to taste. Set aside to cool.

4 Hull the strawberries and halve if necessary. Toss with the pasta and transfer to a serving bowl.

5 Spread the almonds on a baking sheet and toast under the broiler until golden. Cool.

6 Stir the kirsch into the raspberry sauce and pour over the salad. Scatter with the toasted almonds and serve.

PIZZA PRESTO

The pizza originated as a cheap, savory snack in Naples, sold from street stalls or in special eating houses, but it has long since been upgraded to a universally popular main meal. Today's favorite fast food, pizzas are quick and filling meals for people in a hurry. If you make your own you will find they are quick, easy and fun – the simplest are often the best. They are suitable for all tastes, with toppings that have become far more generous and varied than the traditional Italian pizzas.

In this section you will find instructions on how to make basic pizza dough as well as several delicious alternatives. The amount of dough needed for one recipe is small and very easy to handle, and preparations are simple and straightforward. If using readymade bases, these recipes can be made even more speedily, and are ideal if you are short of time.

A word on baking pizzas: the very best results are achieved by cooking them in a traditional brick oven to make them light and crisp. Even without a brick oven, the home cook can achieve excellent results with a pizza stone and it is well worth buying one if you make pizzas frequently. The direct heat makes them wonderfully crisp. Pizzas must be eaten straight from the oven as they soon harden in an unappetizing way.

Pizzas need not be served just as snacks or main meals; they can become stylish appetizers, when they are made as small pizzettes or served in thin wedges. They also make great party food – a festive array of pizzas will please any crowd!

This is a collection for pizza lovers everywhere. Although most of the recipes contain cheese, this can be reduced if you desire a lighter pizza. There is also a final chapter of interesting Italian breads, full of great flavors and textures just waiting to be tasted.

Basic Pizza Dough

This simple bread base is rolled out thinly for a
traditional pizza recipe.

MAKES
1 × 10–12 in round pizza
    base
4 × 5 in round pizza bases
1 × 12 × 7 in oblong pizza
    base

INGREDIENTS
1½ cups bread flour
¼ tsp salt
1 tsp rapid-rise dried yeast
½–⅔ cups lukewarm water
1 tbsp olive oil

1 Sift the flour and salt into a large mixing bowl.

2 Stir in the yeast.

3 Make a well in the center of the dry ingredients. Pour in the water and oil and mix with a spoon to a soft dough.

4 Knead the dough on a lightly floured surface for about 10 minutes until smooth and elastic.

5 Place the dough in a greased bowl and cover with plastic wrap. Let rise in a warm place for about 1 hour or until the dough has doubled in size.

6 Punch down the dough. Turn on to a lightly floured surface and knead again for 2–3 minutes. Roll out as required and place on a greased baking sheet. Pinch up the dough to make a rim. The dough is now ready for topping.

Deep-dish Pizza Dough

This recipe produces a deep and spongy base.

MAKES
1 × 10 in deep-dish pizza base

INGREDIENTS
2 cups bread flour
½ tsp salt
1 tsp rapid-rise dried yeast
⅔ cup lukewarm water
2 tbsp olive oil

Follow the method for Basic Pizza Dough. When the dough has doubled in size, punch down and knead for 2–3 minutes. Roll out the dough to fit a greased 10 in deep-dish pizza pan or square cake pan. Let the dough prove for 10 minutes, then add the topping. Alternatively, shape and place on a greased baking sheet.

Whole Wheat Pizza Dough

INGREDIENTS
3 oz/¾ cup whole wheat flour
¾ cup bread flour
¼ tsp salt
1 tsp rapid-rise dried yeast
½–⅔ cup lukewarm water
1 tbsp olive oil

Follow the method for Basic Pizza Dough. You may have to add a little extra water to form a soft dough, depending on the absorbency of the flour.

Cornmeal Pizza Dough

INGREDIENTS
1½ cups bread flour
¼ cup cornmeal
¼ tsp salt
1 tsp rapid-rise dried yeast
½–⅔ cup lukewarm water
1 tbsp olive oil

Follow the method for Basic Pizza Dough.

Scone Pizza Dough

The joy of using a scone mixture is it's quick to make and uses pantry cupboard ingredients.

MAKES
1 × 10 in round pizza base
1 × 12 × 7 in oblong pizza
   base

INGREDIENTS
1 cup self-rising flour
1 cup self-rising whole wheat
   flour
pinch of salt
4 tbsp butter, diced
²⁄₃ cup milk

1 Mix together the flours and salt in a mixing bowl. Rub in the butter until the mixture resembles fine bread crumbs.

2 Add the milk and mix with a wooden spoon to a soft dough.

3 Knead lightly on a lightly floured surface until smooth. The dough is now ready to use.

Superquick Pizza Dough

If you're really pressed for time, try a packaged pizza dough mix. For best results roll out the dough to a 10–12 in circle; this is slightly larger than stated on the package, but it does produce a perfect thin, crispy base. For a deep-dish version use two packets.

ALSO MAKES
4 × 5 in round pizza bases
1 × 12 × 7 in oblong pizza
   base

INGREDIENTS
1 × 5 oz package pizza base mix
½ cup lukewarm water

1 Empty the contents of the package into a mixing bowl.

2 Pour in the water and mix with a wooden spoon to a soft dough.

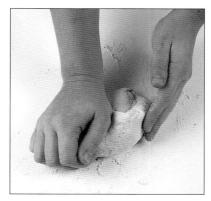

3 Turn the dough on to a lightly floured surface and knead for 5 minutes until smooth and elastic. The dough is now ready to use.

Using a Food Processor

For speed make the pizza dough in a food processor; let the machine do the mixing and kneading, then let the dough proof until doubled in size.

1 Put the flour, salt and yeast into a food processor. Process to mix for a few seconds.

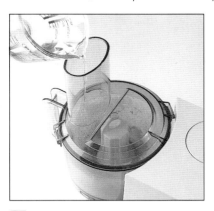

2 Measure the water into a bowl and add the oil. With the machine running, add the liquid and process until the dough forms a soft ball. Leave to rest for 2 minutes, then process for 1 minute more to knead the dough.

3 Remove the dough from the processor and shape into a neat round. Place in a greased bowl and cover with plastic wrap. Let rise in a warm place for about 1 hour until doubled in size. Punch down and knead the dough for 2–3 minutes. The dough is now ready to use.

Readymade Pizza Bases

Fortunately for the busy cook it is now possible to buy fresh, frozen or long-life pizza bases from most supermarkets. Many are enriched with additional ingredients like cheese, herbs and onions. Although they never seem to taste as good as a real homemade pizza base they can be very useful to keep on hand. All you have to do is add your chosen topping and bake in the usual way.

Pitting Olives

Using a pitter is the easiest way to remove the pit from an olive, but you can also use a sharp knife.

1 Put the olive in the pitter, pointed end uppermost.

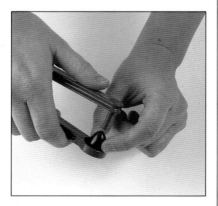

2 Squeeze the handles together to extract the pit.

Chopping Herbs

Use this method to chop herbs until they are as coarse or fine as you wish.

1 Strip the leaves from the stem and pile them on a cutting board.

2 Using a sharp knife cut the herbs into small pieces, holding the tip of the blade against the board and rocking the blade back and forth.

Tomato Sauce

Tomato sauce forms the basis of the topping in many of the recipes. Make sure it is well seasoned and thick before spreading it over the base. It will keep fresh in a covered container in the fridge for up to 3 days.

COVERS
1 × 10–12 in round pizza
   base
1 × 12 × 7 in oblong pizza
   base

INGREDIENTS
1 tbsp olive oil
1 onion, finely chopped
1 garlic clove, crushed
1 × 14 oz can chopped tomatoes
1 tbsp tomato paste
1 tbsp chopped fresh mixed herbs,
   such as parsley, thyme, basil and
   oregano
pinch of sugar
salt and black pepper

1 Heat the oil in a pan, add the onion and garlic and gently sauté for about 5 minutes until softened.

2 Add the tomatoes, tomato paste, herbs, sugar and seasoning.

3 Simmer, uncovered, stirring occasionally for 15–20 minutes or until the tomatoes have reduced to a thick pulp. Leave to cool.

Flavored Oils

For extra flavor brush these over the pizza base before adding the topping. They also form a kind of protective seal that keeps the crust crisp and dry.

CHILI

INGREDIENTS
⅔ cup olive oil
2 tsp tomato paste
1 tbsp dried red chili flakes

1 Heat the oil in a pan until very hot but not smoking. Stir in the tomato paste and red chili flakes. Leave to cool.

2 Pour the chili oil into a small jar or bottle. Cover and store in the fridge for up to one week.

GARLIC

INGREDIENTS
3–4 whole garlic cloves
½ cup olive oil

1 Peel the garlic cloves and put them into a small jar or bottle.

2 Pour in the oil, cover and refrigerate for up to 1 week.

Margherita

(Tomato, Basil and Mozzarella)
This classic pizza is simple to prepare. The sweet flavor of sun-ripened tomatoes works wonderfully with the basil and mozzarella.

Serves 2–3

INGREDIENTS
1 pizza base, about 10–12 in
   diameter
2 tbsp olive oil
1 quantity Tomato Sauce
5 oz mozzarella
2 ripe tomatoes, thinly sliced
6–8 fresh basil leaves
2 tbsp freshly grated Parmesan
black pepper

basil

mozzarella

Parmesan

olive oil

tomatoes

Tomato Sauce

1 Preheat the oven to 425°F. Brush the pizza base with 1 tbsp of the oil and then spread over the Tomato Sauce.

2 Cut the mozzarella into thin slices.

3 Arrange the sliced mozzarella and tomatoes on top of the pizza base.

4 Roughly tear the basil leaves, add and sprinkle with the Parmesan. Drizzle over the remaining oil and season with black pepper. Bake for 15–20 minutes until crisp and golden. Serve immediately.

Marinara

(Tomato and Garlic)
The combination of garlic, good quality olive oil and oregano give this pizza an unmistakably Italian flavor.

Serves 2–3

INGREDIENTS
4 tbsp olive oil
1½ lb plum tomatoes, peeled, seeded and chopped
1 pizza base, about 10–12 in diameter
4 garlic cloves, cut into slivers
1 tbsp chopped fresh oregano
salt and black pepper

olive oil

oregano

plum tomatoes

garlic

1 Preheat the oven to 425°F. Heat 2 tbsp of the oil in a pan. Add the tomatoes and cook, stirring frequently for about 5 minutes until soft.

2 Place the tomatoes in a strainer and leave to drain for about 5 minutes.

3 Transfer the tomatoes to a food processor or blender and purée until smooth.

4 Brush the pizza base with half the remaining oil. Spoon over the tomatoes and sprinkle with garlic and oregano. Drizzle over the remaining oil and season. Bake for 15–20 minutes until crisp and golden. Serve immediately.

Quattro Stagioni

(Four Seasons)
This traditional pizza is divided into quarters, each with a different topping to depict the four seasons of the year.

Serves 2–4

INGREDIENTS
3 tbsp olive oil
2 oz mushrooms, sliced
1 pizza base, about 10–12 in
    diameter
1 quantity Tomato Sauce
2 oz prosciutto
6 pitted black olives, chopped
4 bottled artichoke hearts in oil,
    drained
3 canned anchovy fillets, drained
2 oz mozzarella, thinly sliced
8 fresh basil leaves, shredded
black pepper

artichoke hearts

mozzarella

olive oil

Tomato Sauce

prosciutto

basil

black olives

mushrooms

anchovy fillets

1 Preheat the oven to 425°F. Heat 1 tbsp of the oil in a frying pan and fry the mushrooms until all the juices have evaporated. Leave to cool.

2 Brush the pizza base with half the remaining oil. Spread over the Tomato Sauce and mark into four equal sections with a knife.

3 Arrange the mushrooms over one section of the pizza.

4 Cut the prosciutto into strips and arrange with the olives on another section.

5 Thinly slice the artichoke hearts and arrange over a third section. Halve the anchovies lengthwise and arrange with the mozzarella over the fourth section.

6 Sprinkle the basil over. Drizzle the remaining oil over and season with black pepper. Bake for 15–20 minutes until crisp and golden. Serve immediately.

Napoletana

(Tomato, Mozzarella and Anchovies)
This pizza is a speciality of Naples. It is both one of the
simplest to prepare and the most tasty.

Serves 2–3

INGREDIENTS
1 pizza base, about 10–12 in
    diameter
2 tbsp olive oil
6 plum tomatoes
2 garlic cloves, chopped
4 oz mozzarella, grated
2 oz can anchovy fillets, drained and
    chopped
1 tbsp chopped fresh oregano
2 tbsp freshly grated Parmesan
black pepper

Parmesan

mozzarella

anchovy fillets

olive oil

plum tomatoes

garlic

oregano

1 Preheat the oven to 425°F. Brush the
pizza base with 1 tbsp of the oil. Put the
tomatoes in a bowl and pour over boiling
water. Leave for 30 seconds, then plunge
into cold water.

2 Peel, seed and coarsely chop the
tomatoes. Spoon the tomatoes over the
pizza base and sprinkle over the garlic.

3 Mix the mozzarella with the
anchovies and sprinkle over.

4 Sprinkle over the oregano and
Parmesan. Drizzle over the remaining oil
and season with black pepper. Bake for
15–20 minutes until crisp and golden.
Serve immediately.

Quattro Formaggi

(Four Cheeses)

Rich and tasty, these individual pizzas are quick to assemble, and the aroma of melting cheese is irresistible.

Serves 4

INGREDIENTS
1 quantity Basic or Superquick Pizza
    Dough
1 tbsp Garlic Oil
½ small red onion, very thinly sliced
2 oz Saga Blue
2 oz mozzarella
2 oz Gruyère, grated
2 tbsp freshly grated Parmesan
1 tbsp chopped fresh thyme
black pepper

mozzarella

red onion

Parmesan

Garlic Oil

Saga Blue

Gruyère

thyme

1 Preheat the oven to 425°F. Divide the dough into four pieces and roll out each one on a lightly floured surface into a 5 in circle. Place well apart on two greased baking sheets, then pinch up the dough edges to make a thin rim. Brush with Garlic Oil and top with the red onion.

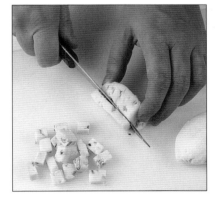

2 Cut the Saga Blue and mozzarella into cubes and scatter over the bases.

3 Mix together the Gruyère, Parmesan and thyme and sprinkle over.

4 Grind over plenty of black pepper. Bake for 15–20 minutes until crisp and golden and the cheese is bubbling. Serve immediately.

Fiorentina

Spinach is the star ingredient of this pizza. A grating of nutmeg to heighten its flavor gives this pizza its unique character.

Serves 2–3

INGREDIENTS
6 oz fresh spinach
3 tbsp olive oil
1 small red onion, thinly sliced
1 pizza base, about 10–12 in
   diameter
1 quantity Tomato Sauce
freshly grated nutmeg
5 oz mozzarella
1 large egg
1 oz Gruyere, grated

mozzarella

Gruyère

Tomato Sauce

spinach

red onion

nutmeg

egg

1 Preheat the oven to 425°F. Remove the stems from the spinach and wash the leaves in plenty of cold water. Drain well and pat dry with paper towels.

2 Heat 1 tbsp of the oil and fry the onion until soft. Add the spinach and continue to fry until just wilted. Drain off any excess liquid.

3 Brush the pizza base with half the remaining oil. Spread over the Tomato Sauce, then top with the spinach mixture. Grate some nutmeg over.

4 Thinly slice the mozzarella and arrange over the spinach. Drizzle the remaining oil over. Bake for 10 minutes, then remove from the oven.

5 Make a small well in the center and drop the egg into the hole.

6 Sprinkle over the Gruyère and return to the oven for a further 5–10 minutes until crisp and golden. Serve immediately.

American Hot

This popular pizza is spiced with green chilies and pepperoni.

Serves 2–3

INGREDIENTS
1 pizza base, about 10–12 in
    diameter
1 tbsp olive oil
4 oz can peeled and chopped green
    chilies in brine, drained
1 quantity Tomato Sauce
3 oz sliced pepperoni
6 pitted black olives
1 tbsp chopped fresh oregano
4 oz mozzarella, grated
oregano leaves, to garnish

mozzarella

oregano

Tomato Sauce

pepperoni

olive oil

green chillies

black olives

1 Preheat the oven to 425°F. Brush the pizza base with the oil.

2 Stir the chilies into the sauce, and spread over the base.

3 Sprinkle the pepperoni over.

4 Halve the olives lengthwise and sprinkle over, with the oregano.

5 Sprinkle the grated mozzarella over and bake for 15–20 minutes until the pizza is crisp and golden.

VARIATION

You can make this pizza as hot as you like. For a really fiery version use fresh red or green chilies, cut into thin slices, in place of the chilies in brine.

6 Garnish with oregano leaves and serve immediately.

Prosciutto, Mushroom and Artichoke

Here is a pizza full of rich and varied flavors. For a delicious variation use mixed cultivated mushrooms.

Serves 2–3

INGREDIENTS
1 bunch scallions
4 tbsp olive oil
8 oz mushrooms, sliced
2 garlic cloves, chopped
1 pizza base, about 10–12 in
    diameter
8 slices prosciutto
4 bottled artichoke hearts in oil,
    drained and sliced
4 tbsp freshly grated Parmesan
salt and black pepper
thyme sprigs, to garnish

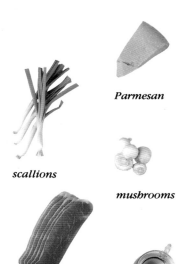

scallions

Parmesan

mushrooms

prosciutto

olive oil

artichoke hearts

1 Preheat the oven to 425°F. Trim the scallions, then chop all the white and some of the green stems.

2 Heat 2 tbsp of the oil in a frying pan. Add the scallions, mushrooms and garlic and fry over a moderate heat until all the juices have evaporated. Season and let cool.

3 Brush the pizza base with half the remaining oil. Arrange the prosciutto, mushrooms and artichoke hearts on top.

4 Sprinkle the Parmesan over, then drizzle the remaining oil over and season. Bake for 15–20 minutes. Garnish with thyme sprigs and serve immediately.

Chorizo and Corn

The combination of spicy chorizo and sweet, tender corn works well in this hearty and colorful pizza. For a simple variation you could use chopped fresh basil instead of Italian parsley.

Serves 2–3

INGREDIENTS

1 pizza base, about 10–12 in diameter
1 tbsp Garlic Oil
1 quantity Tomato Sauce
6 oz chorizo sausages
6 oz (drained weight) canned corn kernels
2 tbsp chopped fresh Italian parsley
2 oz mozzarella, grated
2 tbsp freshly grated Parmesan

Tomato Sauce

mozzarella

Italian parsley

Garlic Oil

chorizo sausages

Parmesan

1 Preheat the oven to 425°F. Brush the pizza base with Garlic Oil and spread over the Tomato Sauce.

2 Skin and cut the chorizo sausages into chunks and scatter over the Tomato Sauce. Bake for 10 minutes then remove from the oven.

3 Sprinkle over the corn and Italian parsley.

4 Mix together the mozzarella and Parmesan and sprinkle over. Bake for a further 5–10 minutes until crisp and golden. Serve immediately.

sweetcorn

Beef Chili

Ground beef, red kidney beans and smoky cheese combined with oregano, cumin and chilies give this pizza a Mexican character.

Serves 4

INGREDIENTS
2 tbsp olive oil
1 red onion, finely chopped
1 garlic clove, crushed
½ red bell pepper, seeded and finely chopped
6 oz lean ground beef
½ tsp ground cumin
2 fresh red chilies, seeded and chopped
4 oz (drained weight) canned red kidney beans
1 quantity Cornmeal Pizza Dough
1 quantity Tomato Sauce
1 tbsp chopped fresh oregano
2 oz mozzarella, grated
3 oz smoked Cheddar, grated
salt and black pepper

Tomato Sauce

red onion

ground beef

mozzarella

smoked Cheddar

red chilies

oregano

olive oil

red kidney beans

red bell peppers

1 Preheat the oven to 425°F. Heat 1 tbsp of the oil in a frying pan, add the onion, garlic and pepper and gently fry until soft. Increase the heat, add the beef and brown well, stirring constantly.

2 Add the cumin and chilies and continue to cook, stirring, for about 5 minutes. Add the beans and seasoning.

3 Roll out the dough on a surface dusted with cornmeal and use to line a 12 × 7 in greased jelly roll pan. Pinch up the dough edges to make a rim.

4 Spread the Tomato Sauce over.

5 Spoon the beef mixture over then sprinkle the oregano over.

6 Sprinkle the cheeses over and bake for 15–20 minutes until crisp and golden. Serve immediately.

VARIATION

If you prefer a milder version of this spicy pizza, reduce the amount of fresh chilies or leave them out altogether.

Chicken, Shiitake Mushroom and Cilantro

The addition of shiitake mushrooms adds an earthy flavor to this colorful pizza, while fresh red chili provides a hint of spiciness.

Serves 3–4

INGREDIENTS
3 tbsp olive oil
12 oz chicken breast fillets, skinned
    and cut into thin strips
1 bunch scallions, sliced
1 fresh red chili, seeded and chopped
1 red bell pepper, seeded and cut into
    thin strips
3 oz fresh shiitake mushrooms, wiped
    and sliced
3–4 tbsp chopped fresh cilantro
1 pizza base, about 10–12 in
    diameter
1 tbsp Chili Oil
5 oz mozzarella
salt and black pepper

chicken breast fillets

scallions

red chili

cilantro

red bell pepper

Chili Oil

olive oil

shiitake mushrooms

1 Preheat the oven to 425°F. Heat 2 tbsp of the olive oil in a wok or large frying pan. Add the chicken, scallions, chili, pepper and mushrooms and stir-fry over a high heat for 2–3 minutes until the chicken is firm but still slightly pink within. Season to taste.

2 Pour off any excess oil, then set aside the chicken mixture to cool.

3 Stir the fresh cilantro into the chicken mixture.

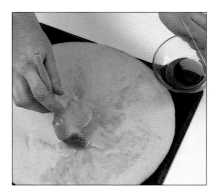

4 Brush the pizza base with the chili oil.

5 Spoon the chicken mixture over and drizzle the remaining olive oil over.

6 Grate the mozzarella and sprinkle over. Bake for 15–20 minutes until crisp and golden. Serve immediately.

Pancetta, Leek and Smoked Mozzarella

Smoked mozzarella with its brownish smoky-flavored skin, pancetta and leeks make this an extremely tasty and easy-to-prepare pizza, ideal for a light lunch.

Serves 4

INGREDIENTS
2 tbsp freshly grated Parmesan
1 quantity Basic or Superquick Pizza
   Dough
2 tbsp olive oil
2 medium leeks
8–12 slices pancetta
5 oz smoked mozzarella
black pepper

pancetta

leeks

smoked mozzarella

olive oil

Parmesan

1 Preheat the oven to 425°F. Dust the work surface with the Parmesan, then knead into the dough. Divide the dough into four pieces and roll out each one to a 5 in circle. Place well apart on two greased baking sheets, then pinch up the edges to make a thin rim. Brush with 1 tbsp of the oil.

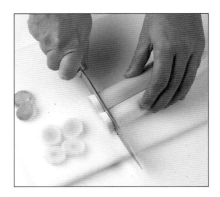

2 Trim and thinly slice the leeks.

3 Arrange the pancetta and leeks on the pizza bases.

4 Grate the smoked mozzarella and sprinkle over. Drizzle the remaining oil over and season with black pepper. Bake for 15–20 minutes until crisp and golden. Serve immediately.

Ham and Mozzarella Calzone

A calzone is a kind of "inside-out" pizza – the dough is on the outside and the filling on the inside. For a vegetarian version replace the ham with sautéed mushrooms or chopped cooked spinach.

Serves 2

INGREDIENTS

1 quantity Basic or Superquick Pizza Dough
4 oz ricotta
2 tbsp freshly grated Parmesan
1 egg yolk
2 tbsp chopped fresh basil
3 oz cooked ham, finely chopped
3 oz mozzarella, cut into small cubes
olive oil for brushing
salt and black pepper

basil

ricotta

egg

mozzarella

Parmesan

cooked ham

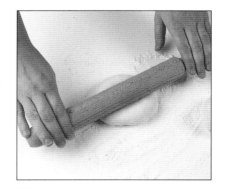

1 Preheat the oven to 425°F. Divide the dough in to two pieces and roll out each piece on a lightly floured surface to a 7 in circle.

2 In a bowl mix together the ricotta, Parmesan, egg yolk, basil and seasoning.

3 Spread the mixture over half of each circle, leaving a 1 in border, then scatter the ham and mozzarella on top. Dampen the edges with water, then fold over the other half of dough to enclose the filling.

4 Press the edges firmly together to seal. Place on two greased baking sheets. Brush with oil and make a small hole in the top of each to allow the steam to escape. Bake for 15–20 minutes until golden. Serve immediately.

Smoked Chicken, Yellow Pepper and Sun-dried Tomato Pizzettes

These ingredients complement each other perfectly and make a really delicious topping.

Serves 4

INGREDIENTS

1 quantity Basic or Superquick Pizza
  Dough
3 tbsp olive oil
4 tbsp sun-dried tomato paste
2 yellow bell peppers, seeded and cut
  into thin strips
6 oz sliced smoked chicken or turkey,
  chopped
5 oz mozzarella, cubed
2 tbsp chopped fresh basil
salt and black pepper

basil

mozzarella

yellow bell peppers

olive oil

smoked chicken

sun-dried tomato paste

1 Preheat the oven to 425°F Divide the dough into four pieces and roll out each one on a lightly floured surface to a 5 in circle. Place well apart on two greased baking sheets, then pinch up the dough edges to make a thin rim. Brush with 1 tbsp of the oil.

2 Brush the pizza bases generously with the sun-dried tomato paste.

3 Stir-fry the peppers in half the remaining oil for 3–4 minutes.

4 Arrange the chicken and peppers on top of the sun-dried tomato paste.

5 Scatter the mozzarella and basil over. Season with salt and black pepper.

VARIATION

For a vegetarian pizza with a similar smoky taste, omit the chicken, roast the yellow peppers and remove the skins before using, and replace the mozzarella with Gouda smoked cheese.

6 Drizzle over the remaining oil and bake for 15–20 minutes until crisp and golden. Serve immediately.

Spicy Sausage

This is a tasty and substantial pizza. You may substitute fresh Italian spicy sausages, available from good Italian delicatessens, if you prefer.

Serves 3–4

INGREDIENTS
8 oz good quality pork sausages
1 tsp mild chili powder
½ tsp freshly ground black pepper
2 tbsp olive oil
2–3 garlic cloves
1 pizza base, about 10–12 in
    diameter
1 quantity Tomato Sauce
1 red onion, thinly sliced
1 tbsp chopped fresh oregano
1 tbsp chopped fresh thyme
2 oz mozzarella, grated
2 oz freshly grated Parmesan

Tomato Sauce

thyme and oregano

red onion   *Parmesan*

mozzarella

olive oil

pork sausages

mild chili powder

1 Preheat the oven to 425°F. Skin the sausages by running a sharp knife down the side of the skins. Place the sausage meat in a bowl and add the chili powder and black pepper; mix well. Break the sausage meat mixture into walnut-sized balls.

2 Heat 1 tbsp of the oil in a frying pan and fry the sausage balls for 2–3 minutes until evenly browned.

3 Using a slotted spoon remove the sausage balls from the pan and drain on paper towels.

4 Thinly slice the garlic cloves.

5 Brush the pizza base with the remaining oil, then spread over the Tomato Sauce. Scatter the sausages, garlic, onion and herbs over.

6 Sprinkle over the mozzarella and Parmesan and bake for 15–20 minutes until crisp and golden. Serve immediately.

Caramelized Onion, Salami and Black Olive

The flavor of the sweet caramelized onion is offset by the salty black olives and herbes de Provence in the pizza base and the sprinkling of Parmesan to finish.

Serves 4

INGREDIENTS
1 ½ lb red onions
4 tbsp olive oil
12 pitted black olives
1 quantity Basic or Superquick Pizza
   Dough
1 tsp dried herbes de Provence
6–8 slices Italian salami, quartered
2–3 tbsp freshly grated Parmesan
black pepper

Italian salami

olive oil

red onions

Parmesan

black olives

herbes de Provence

1 Preheat the oven to 425°F. Thinly slice the onions.

2 Heat 2 tbsp of the oil in a pan and add the onions. Cover and cook gently for 15–20 minutes, stirring occasionally until the onions are soft and very lightly colored. Leave to cool.

3 Finely chop the black olives.

4 Knead the dough on a lightly floured surface, adding the black olives and herbes de Provence. Roll out the dough and use to line a 12 × 7 in jelly roll pan. Pinch up the dough edges to make a thin rim and brush with half the remaining oil.

5 Spoon half the onions over the base, top with the salami and the remaining onions.

6 Grind over plenty of black pepper and drizzle over the remaining oil. Bake for 15–20 minutes until crisp and golden. Remove from the oven and sprinkle the Parmesan over to serve.

Ham and Pineapple French Bread Pizza

French bread makes a great pizza base. For a really speedy recipe use ready-made pizza topping instead of the Tomato Sauce.

Serves 4

INGREDIENTS
2 small baguettes
1 quantity Tomato Sauce
3 oz sliced cooked ham
4 rings canned pineapple, drained well and chopped
½ small green bell pepper, seeded and cut into thin strips
3 oz sharp Cheddar
salt and black pepper

sharp Cheddar

green bell pepper

pineapple

cooked ham

baguette

Tomato Sauce

1 Preheat the oven to 400°F. Cut the baguettes in half lengthwise and toast the cut sides until crisp and golden.

2 Spread the Tomato Sauce over the toasted baguettes.

3 Cut the ham into strips and arrange on the baguettes with the pineapple and pepper. Season.

4 Grate the Cheddar and sprinkle on top. Bake or broil for 15–20 minutes until crisp and golden.

Prosciutto, Roasted Bell Peppers and Mozzarella Pizzas

Succulent roasted peppers, salty prosciutto and creamy mozzarella – the delicious flavors of these easy pizzas are hard to beat.

Serves 2

INGREDIENTS
½ loaf country bread
1 red bell pepper, roasted and peeled
1 yellow bell pepper, roasted and peeled
4 slices prosciutto, cut into thick strips
3 oz mozzarella
black pepper
tiny basil leaves, to garnish

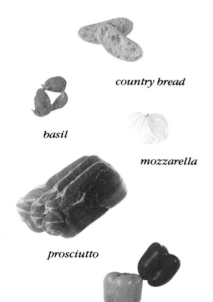

country bread

basil

mozzarella

prosciutto

red and yellow bell peppers

1 Cut the bread into four thick slices and toast both sides until golden.

2 Cut the roasted peppers into thick strips and arrange on the toasted bread with the prosciutto.

3 Thinly slice the mozzarella and arrange on top. Grind plenty of black pepper over. Place under a hot broiler for 2–3 minutes.

4 Arrange the basil leaves on top and serve immediately.

Pepperoni Pan Pizza

This pizza is made using a scone base which happily does not require proving! The topping can be varied to include whatever you like best – tunafish, shrimp, ham or salami are all good alternatives to the pepperoni.

Serves 2–3

INGREDIENTS

1 tbsp chopped fresh mixed herbs
1 quantity Scone Pizza Dough
2 tbsp tomato paste
14 oz can crushed tomatoes, drained well
2 oz mushrooms, thinly sliced
3 oz sliced pepperoni
6 pitted black olives, chopped
2 oz Edam, grated
2 oz sharp Cheddar, grated
1 tbsp chopped fresh basil, to garnish

sharp Cheddar

Edam

mushrooms

chopped tomatoes

black olives

basil

fresh mixed herbs

pepperoni

tomato paste

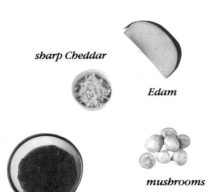

1 Add the herbs to the scone mix before mixing to a soft dough.

2 Turn the dough on to a lightly floured surface and knead lightly until smooth. Roll out to fit a well-greased frying pan, about 8½ in diameter.

3 Cook the dough in the pan over a low heat for about 5 minutes until the base is golden. Lift carefully with a spatula to check.

4 Turn the base on to a baking sheet, then slide it back into the pan, with the cooked side uppermost.

5 Mix together the tomato paste and drained tomatoes and spread over the pizza base. Scatter over the mushrooms, pepperoni, olives and cheeses. Continue to cook for about 5 minutes until the underside is golden.

6 When it is ready, transfer the pan to a preheated moderate broiler for 4–5 minutes to melt the cheese. Scatter the basil over and serve immediately.

Mixed Seafood

Here is a pizza that gives you the full flavor of the Mediterranean, ideal for a summer evening supper!

Serves 3–4

INGREDIENTS
1 pizza base, 10–12 in diameter
2 tbsp olive oil
1 quantity Tomato Sauce
14 oz mixed cooked seafood
   (including mussels, shrimp and
   squid)
3 garlic cloves
2 tbsp chopped fresh parsley
2 tbsp freshly grated Parmesan, to
   garnish

mixed seafood

garlic

olive oil

parsley

Tomato Sauce

Parmesan

1 Preheat the oven to 425°F. Brush the pizza base with 1 tbsp of the oil.

2 Spread the Tomato Sauce over. Bake in the oven for 10 minutes. Remove from the oven.

3 Pat the seafood dry using paper towels, then arrange on top.

4 Chop the garlic and sprinkle over.

5 Sprinkle the parsley over, then drizzle the remaining oil over.

VARIATION

If you prefer, this pizza can be made with mussels or shrimp on their own, or any combination of your favorite seafood.

6 Bake for a further 5–10 minutes until the seafood is warmed through and the base is crisp and golden. Sprinkle with Parmesan and serve immediately.

Salmon and Avocado

Smoked and fresh salmon make a delicious pizza topping when mixed with avocado. Smoked salmon trimmings are cheaper than smoked salmon slices and could be used instead.

Serves 3–4

INGREDIENTS

5 oz salmon fillet
½ cup dry white wine
1 pizza base, 10–12 in diameter
1 tbsp olive oil
14 oz can chopped tomatoes, drained well
4 oz mozzarella, grated
1 small avocado
2 tsp lemon juice
2 tbsp crème fraîche
3 oz smoked salmon, cut into strips
1 tbsp capers
2 tbsp chopped fresh chives, to garnish
black pepper

lemon

dry white wine

chopped tomatoes

mozzarella

avocado

smoked salmon

salmon fillet

crème fraîche

1 Preheat the oven to 425°F. Place the salmon fillet in a frying pan, pour the wine over and season with black pepper. Bring slowly to a boil, remove from the heat, cover and cool. (The fish will continue to cook in the cooling liquid.) Skin and flake the salmon into small pieces, removing any bones.

2 Brush the pizza base with the oil and spread over the drained tomatoes. Sprinkle 2 oz of the mozzarella over. Bake for 10 minutes, then remove from the oven.

3 Meanwhile, halve, pit and peel the avocado. Cut the flesh into small cubes and toss carefully in the lemon juice.

4 Dot teaspoonsful of the crème fraîche over the pizza base.

5 Arrange the fresh and smoked salmon, avocado, capers and remaining mozzarella on top. Season with black pepper. Bake for a further 5–10 minutes until crisp and golden.

6 Sprinkle the chives over and serve immediately.

Shrimp, Sun-dried Tomato and Basil Pizzettes

Sun-dried tomatoes with their concentrated caramelized tomato flavor make an excellent topping for pizzas. Serve these pretty pizzettes as an appetizer or snack.

Serves 4

INGREDIENTS
1 quantity Basic or Superquick Pizza
   Dough
2 tbsp Chili Oil
3 oz mozzarella, grated
1 garlic clove, chopped
½ small red onion, thinly sliced
4–6 pieces sun-dried tomatoes, thinly
   sliced
4 oz cooked shrimp, peeled
2 tbsp chopped fresh basil
salt and black pepper
shredded basil leaves, to garnish

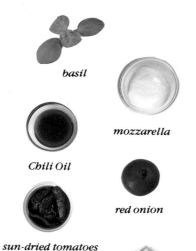

basil

Chili Oil

mozzarella

red onion

sun-dried tomatoes

garlic

1 Preheat the oven to 425°F. Divide the dough into eight pieces.

2 Roll out each one on a lightly floured surface to a small oval about ¼ in thick. Place well apart on two greased baking sheets. Prick all over with a fork.

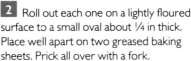

3 Brush the pizza bases with 1 tbsp of the chili oil and top with the mozzarella, leaving a ½ in border.

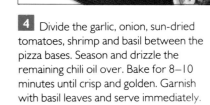

4 Divide the garlic, onion, sun-dried tomatoes, shrimp and basil between the pizza bases. Season and drizzle the remaining chili oil over. Bake for 8–10 minutes until crisp and golden. Garnish with basil leaves and serve immediately.

Crab and Parmesan Calzonelli

These miniature calzone owe their popularity to their impressive presentation. If preferred, you can use shrimp instead of crab.

Makes 10–12

INGREDIENTS
1 quantity Basic or Superquick Pizza Dough
4 oz mixed prepared crabmeat, defrosted if frozen
1 tbsp heavy cream
2 tbsp freshly grated Parmesan
2 tbsp chopped fresh parsley
1 garlic clove, crushed
salt and black pepper
parsley sprigs, to garnish

Parmesan

heavy cream

crabmeat

parsley

garlic

1 Preheat the oven to 400°F. Roll out the dough on a lightly floured surface to ⅛ in thick. Using a 3 in plain round cutter stamp out 10–12 circles.

2 In a bowl mix together the crabmeat, cream, Parmesan, parsley, garlic and seasoning.

3 Spoon a little of the filling on to one half of each circle. Dampen the edges with water and fold over to enclose filling.

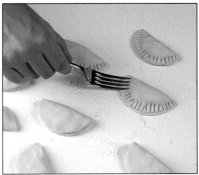

4 Seal the edges by pressing with a fork. Place well apart on two greased baking sheets. Bake for 10–15 minutes until golden. Garnish with parsley sprigs.

Mussel and Leek Pizzettes

Serve these tasty seafood pizzettes with a crisp green salad for a light lunch.

Serves 4

INGREDIENTS
1 lb live mussels
½ cup dry white wine
1 quantity Basic or Superquick Pizza
   Dough
1 tbsp olive oil
2 oz Gruyère
2 oz mozzarella
2 small leeks
salt and black pepper

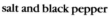

dry white wine

olive oil

mozzarella

mussels

Gruyère

leeks

1 Preheat the oven to 425°F. Place the mussels in a bowl of cold water to soak, and scrub well. Remove the beards and discard any mussels that are open.

2 Place the mussels in a pan. Pour over the wine, cover and cook over a high heat, shaking the pan occasionally, for 5–10 minutes until the mussels have opened.

3 Drain off the cooking liquid. Remove the mussels from their shells, discarding any that remain closed. Leave to cool.

4 Divide the dough into four pieces and roll out each one on a lightly floured surface to a 5 in circle. Place well apart on two greased baking sheets, then pinch up the dough edges to form a thin rim. Brush the pizza bases with the oil. Grate the cheeses and sprinkle half evenly over the bases.

5 Thinly slice the leeks, then scatter over the cheese. Bake for 10 minutes, then remove from the oven.

VARIATION

Frozen or canned mussels can also be used, but will not have the same flavor and texture. Make sure you defrost the mussels properly.

6 Arrange the mussels on top. Season and sprinkle the remaining cheese over. Bake for a further 5–10 minutes until crisp and golden. Serve immediately.

Anchovy, Pepper and Tomato

This pretty, summery pizza is utterly simple, yet quite delicious. It's well worth broiling the peppers as they take on a subtle smoky flavor.

Serves 2–3

INGREDIENTS
6 plum tomatoes
3 tbsp olive oil
1 tsp salt
1 large red bell pepper
1 large yellow bell pepper
1 pizza base, 10–12 in diameter
2 garlic cloves, chopped
2 oz can anchovy fillets, drained and chopped
black pepper
basil leaves, to garnish

olive oil

red and yellow bell peppers

plum tomatoes

garlic

anchovy fillets

1 Halve the tomatoes lengthwise and scoop out the seeds.

2 Coarsely chop the flesh and place in a bowl with 1 tbsp of the oil and the salt. Mix well, then leave to marinate for 30 minutes.

3 Meanwhile, preheat the oven to 425°F. Slice the peppers in half lengthwise and remove the seeds. Place the pepper halves, skin-side up, on a baking sheet and broil until the skins of the peppers are evenly charred.

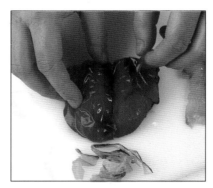

4 Place the peppers in a covered bowl for 10 minutes, then peel off the skins. Cut the flesh into thin strips.

5 Brush the pizza base with half the remaining oil. Drain the tomatoes, then scatter over the base with the peppers and garlic.

6 Sprinkle on the anchovy fillets and season with black pepper. Drizzle over the remaining oil and bake for 15–20 minutes until crisp and golden. Garnish with basil leaves and serve immediately.

Tuna, Anchovy and Caper

This pizza makes a substantial supper dish which will provide two to three generous portions accompanied by a simple salad.

Serves 2–3

INGREDIENTS
1 quantity Scone Pizza Dough
2 tbsp olive oil
1 quantity Tomato Sauce
1 small red onion
7 oz can tuna, drained
1 tbsp capers
12 pitted black olives
3 tbsp freshly grated Parmesan
2 oz can anchovy fillets, drained
    and halved lengthways
black pepper

Tomato Sauce

olive oil

Parmesan

black olives

tuna

red onion

capers

1 Preheat the oven to 425°F. Roll out the dough on a lightly floured surface to a 10 in circle. Place on a greased baking sheet and brush with 1 tbsp of the oil. Spread the Tomato Sauce evenly over the dough.

2 Cut the onion into thin wedges and arrange on top.

3 Coarsely flake the tuna with a fork and scatter the onion over.

4 Sprinkle the capers, black olives and Parmesan over.

5 Lattice the anchovy fillets over the top of the pizza.

6 Drizzle the remaining oil over, then grind over plenty of black pepper. Bake for 15–20 minutes until crisp and golden. Serve immediately.

Roasted Vegetable and Goat Cheese

Here is a pizza which incorporates the smoky flavors of oven-roasted vegetables with the distinctive taste of goat cheese.

Serves 3

INGREDIENTS
1 eggplant, cut into thick chunks
2 small zucchini, sliced lengthwise
1 red bell pepper, quartered and
    seeded
1 yellow bell pepper, quartered and
    seeded
1 small red onion, cut into wedges
6 tbsp Garlic Oil
1 pizza base, 10–12 in diameter
1 × 14 oz can chopped tomatoes,
    drained well
1 × 4 oz goat cheese (with rind)
1 tbsp chopped fresh thyme
black pepper
green olive tapenade, to serve

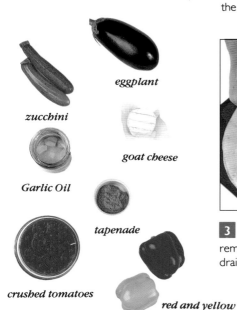

eggplant

zucchini

goat cheese

Garlic Oil

tapenade

crushed tomatoes

red and yellow bell peppers

1 Preheat the oven to 425°F. Place the eggplant, zucchini, peppers and onion in a large roasting pan. Brush with 4 tbsp of the Garlic Oil. Roast for about 30 minutes until lightly charred, turning the peppers halfway through cooking. Remove from the oven and set aside.

2 When the peppers are cool enough to handle, peel off the skins and cut the flesh into thick strips.

3 Brush the pizza base with half the remaining Garlic Oil and spread over the drained tomatoes.

4 Arrange the roasted vegetables on top of the pizza.

5 Cube the goat cheese and arrange on top. Scatter the thyme over.

COOK'S TIP

If you place the roasted peppers in a paper bag while they cool, peeling off the skins becomes easier.

6 Drizzle the remaining Garlic Oil over and season with black pepper. Bake for 15–20 minutes until crisp and golden. Spoon the tapenade over to serve.

New Potato, Rosemary and Garlic

New potatoes, smoked mozzarella, rosemary and garlic make the flavor of this pizza unique. For a delicious variation, use sage instead of rosemary.

Serves 2–3

INGREDIENTS
12 oz new potatoes
3 tbsp olive oil
2 garlic cloves, crushed
1 pizza base, 10–12 in diameter
1 red onion, thinly sliced
5 oz smoked mozzarella, grated
2 tsp chopped fresh rosemary
salt and black pepper
2 tbsp freshly grated Parmesan, to garnish

olive oil

Parmesan

smoked mozzarella

new potatoes

rosemary

red onion

garlic

1 Preheat the oven to 425°F. Cook the potatoes in boiling salted water for 5 minutes. Drain well. When cool, peel and slice thinly.

2 Heat 2 tbsp of the oil in a frying pan. Add the sliced potatoes and garlic and fry for 5–8 minutes until tender.

3 Brush the pizza base with the remaining oil. Scatter the onion over, then arrange the potatoes on top.

4 Sprinkle over the mozzarella and rosemary. Grind over plenty of black pepper and bake for 15–20 minutes until crisp and golden. Remove from the oven and sprinkle the Parmesan over to serve.

Wild Mushroom Pizzettes

Serve these extravagant pizzas as a starter. Fresh wild mushrooms add a distinctive flavor to the topping but a mixture of cultivated mushrooms such as shiitake, oyster and cremini mushrooms would do just as well.

Serves 4

INGREDIENTS
3 tbsp olive oil
12 oz fresh wild mushrooms, washed and sliced
2 shallots, chopped
2 garlic cloves, finely chopped
2 tbsp chopped fresh mixed thyme and Italian parsley
1 quantity Basic or Superquick Pizza Dough
1½ oz Gruyère, grated
2 tbsp freshly grated Parmesan
salt and black pepper

Gruyère

Italian parsley

olive oil

thyme

Parmesan

garlic   *shallots*

wild mushrooms

1 Preheat the oven to 425°F. Heat 2 tbsp of the oil in a frying pan. Add the mushrooms, shallots and garlic and fry over a moderate heat until all the juices have evaporated.

2 Stir in half the herbs and seasoning, then set aside to cool.

3 Divide the dough into four pieces and roll out each one on a lightly floured surface to a 5 in circle. Place well apart on two greased baking sheets, then pinch up the dough edges to form a thin rim. Brush the pizza bases with the remaining oil and top with the wild mushroom mixture.

4 Mix together the Gruyère and Parmesan, then sprinkle over. Bake for 15–20 minutes until crisp and golden. Remove from the oven and sprinkle the remaining herbs over to serve.

Chili, Tomatoes and Spinach

This richly flavored topping with a hint of spice makes a colorful and satisfying pizza.

Serves 3

INGREDIENTS

1–2 fresh red chilies
3 tbsp tomato oil (from jar of sun-
    dried tomatoes)
1 onion, chopped
2 garlic cloves, chopped
2 oz (drained weight) sun-dried
    tomatoes in oil
14 oz can crushed tomatoes
1 tbsp tomato paste
6 oz fresh spinach
1 pizza base, 10–12 in diameter
3 oz smoked Gouda cheese, grated
3 oz sharp Cheddar, grated
salt and black pepper

smoked Gouda cheese

crushed tomatoes

sharp Cheddar

sun-dried tomatoes

onion

garlic

spinach

red chilies

tomato oil

1 Seed and finely chop the chilies.

2 Heat 2 tbsp of the tomato oil in a pan, add the onion, garlic and chilies and gently fry for about 5 minutes until they are soft.

3 Coarsely chop the sun-dried tomatoes. Add to the pan with the crushed tomatoes, tomato paste and seasoning. Simmer uncovered, stirring occasionally, for 15 minutes.

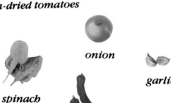

4 Remove the stems from the spinach and wash the leaves in plenty of cold water. Drain well and pat dry with paper towels. Coarsely chop the spinach.

5 Stir the spinach into the sauce. Cook, stirring, for a further 5–10 minutes until the spinach has wilted and no excess moisture remains. Leave to cool.

6 Meanwhile, preheat the oven to 425°F. Brush the pizza base with the remaining tomato oil, then spoon the sauce over. Sprinkle the cheeses over and bake for 15–20 minutes until crisp and golden. Serve immediately.

Tomato, Pesto and Black Olive

These individual pizzas take very little time to put together. Marinating the tomatoes gives them extra flavor.

Serves 4

INGREDIENTS
2 plum tomatoes
1 garlic clove, crushed
4 tbsp olive oil
1 quantity Basic or Superquick Pizza Dough
2 tbsp red pesto
5 oz mozzarella, thinly sliced
4 pitted black olives, chopped
1 tbsp chopped fresh oregano
salt and black pepper
oregano leaves, to garnish

red pesto

mozzarella

oregano

plum tomatoes

black olives

1 Slice the tomatoes thinly crosswise, then cut each slice in half. Place the tomatoes in a shallow dish with the garlic. Drizzle 2 tbsp of the oil over and season. Let marinate for 15 minutes.

2 Meanwhile, preheat the oven to 425°F. Divide the dough into four pieces and roll out each one on a lightly floured surface to a 5 in circle. Place well apart on two greased baking sheets, then pinch up the dough edges to make a rim. Brush the pizza bases with half the remaining oil and spread over the pesto.

3 Drain the tomatoes, then arrange a fan of alternate slices of tomatoes and mozzarella on each base.

4 Sprinkle over the olives and oregano. Drizzle over the remaining oil on top and bake for 15–20 minutes until crisp and golden. Garnish with the oregano leaves and serve immediately.

Fresh Herb

Cut this pizza into thin wedges and serve as part of a mixed antipasti.

Serves 8

INGREDIENTS
4 oz mixed fresh herbs, such as
   parsley, basil and oregano
3 garlic cloves, crushed
½ cup heavy cream
1 pizza base, 10–12 in diameter
1 tbsp Garlic Oil
4 oz Pecorino, grated
salt and black pepper

heavy cream

Garlic Oil

Pecorino

basil

parsley

garlic

1 Preheat the oven to 425°F. Chop the herbs in a food processor if you have one.

2 In a bowl mix together the herbs, garlic, cream and seasoning.

3 Brush the pizza base with the Garlic Oil, then spread the herb mixture over.

4 Sprinkle the Pecorino over. Bake for 15–20 minutes until crisp and golden and the topping is still moist. Cut into thin wedges and serve immediately.

Eggplant, Shallot and Sun-dried Tomato Calzone

Eggplant, shallots and sun-dried tomatoes make an unusual filling for calzone. Add more or less red chili flakes, depending on personal taste.

Serves 2

INGREDIENTS
3 tbsp olive oil
3 shallots, chopped
4 baby eggplants
1 garlic clove, chopped
2 oz (drained weight) sun-dried
   tomatoes in oil, chopped
¼ tsp dried red chilli flakes
2 tsp chopped fresh thyme
1 quantity Basic or Superquick Pizza
   Dough
3 oz mozzarella, cubed
salt and black pepper
1–2 tbsp freshly grated Parmesan, to
   serve

Parmesan

mozzarella

thyme

olive oil

baby eggplants

shallots

red chili flakes

1 Preheat the oven to 425°F. Heat 2 tbsp of the oil in a frying pan. Add the shallots and cook until soft. Trim the eggplants, then cut into small cubes.

2 Add the eggplants to the shallots with the garlic, sun-dried tomatoes, red chili flakes, thyme and seasoning. Cook for 4–5 minutes, stirring frequently, until the eggplant is beginning to soften. Remove from the heat and let cool.

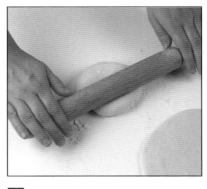

3 Divide the dough in half and roll out each piece on a lightly floured surface to a 7 in circle.

4 Spread the eggplant mixture over half of each circle, leaving a 1 in border, then scatter the mozzarella over.

5 Dampen the edges with water, then fold over the other half of dough to enclose the filling. Press the edges firmly together to seal. Place on two greased baking sheets.

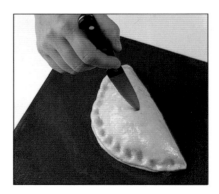

6 Brush with half the remaining oil and make a small hole in the top of each to allow the steam to escape. Bake for 15–20 minutes until golden. Remove from the oven and brush with the remaining oil. Sprinkle the Parmesan over and serve immediately.

Tomato, Fennel and Parmesan

This pizza relies on the winning combination of tomatoes, fennel and Parmesan. The fennel adds both a crisp texture and a distinctive flavor.

Serves 2–3

INGREDIENTS
1 fennel bulb
3 tbsp Garlic Oil
1 pizza base, 10–12 in diameter
1 quantity Tomato Sauce
2 tbsp chopped fresh Italian parsley
2 oz mozzarella, grated
2 oz Parmesan, grated
salt and black pepper

1 Preheat the oven to 425°F. Trim and quarter the fennel lengthwise. Remove the core and slice each quarter of fennel thinly.

Italian parsley

mozzarella

Parmesan

Tomato Sauce

fennel bulb

Garlic Oil

2 Heat 2 tbsp of the Garlic Oil in a frying pan and sauté the fennel for 4–5 minutes until just tender. Season.

3 Brush the pizza base with the remaining Garlic Oil and spread over the Tomato Sauce. Spoon the fennel on top and scatter the Italian parsley over.

4 Mix together the mozzarella and Parmesan and sprinkle over. Bake for 15–20 minutes until crisp and golden. Serve immediately.

Red Onion, Gorgonzola and Sage

This topping combines the richness of Gorgonzola with the earthy flavors of sage and sweet red onions.

Serves 4

INGREDIENTS
1 quantity Basic or Superquick Pizza Dough
2 tbsp Garlic Oil
2 small red onions
5 oz Gorgonzola
2 garlic cloves
2 tsp chopped fresh sage
black pepper

sage

Gorgonzola

garlic

Garlic Oil

red onions

1 Preheat the oven to 425°F. Divide the dough into eight pieces and roll out each one on a lightly floured surface to a small oval about ¼ in thick. Place well apart on two greased baking sheets and prick with a fork. Brush the bases of each oval well with 1 tbsp of the Garlic Oil.

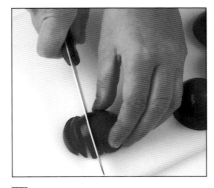

2 Halve, then slice the onions into thin wedges. Scatter over the pizza bases.

3 Remove the rind from the Gorgonzola. Cut the cheese into small cubes, then scatter it over the onions.

4 Cut the garlic lengthwise into thin strips and sprinkle over, along with the sage. Drizzle the remaining oil on top and grind over plenty of black pepper. Bake for 10–15 minutes until crisp and golden. Serve immediately.

Onion and Three Cheese

You can use any combination of cheese you like. Edam and Cheddar both have good flavors and melting properties.

Serves 3–4

INGREDIENTS
3 tbsp olive oil
3 medium onions, sliced
1 pizza base, 10–12 in diameter
4 small tomatoes, peeled, seeded and
   cut into thin wedges
2 tbsp chopped fresh basil
4 oz Saga Blue
5 oz mozzarella
4 oz Red Leicester
black pepper
fresh basil leaves, to garnish

tomatoes

mozzarella

basil

Saga Blue

Red Leicester

olive oil

onions

1 Preheat the oven to 425°F. Heat 2 tbsp of the oil in a frying pan, add the onions and gently fry for about 10 minutes, stirring occasionally. Remove from the heat and let cool.

2 Brush the pizza base with the remaining oil. Spoon the onions and tomatoes over, then scatter the basil leaves over.

3 Thinly slice the cheeses and arrange over the tomatoes and onions.

4 Grind over plenty of black pepper and bake for 15–20 minutes until crisp and golden. Garnish with basil leaves and serve immediately.

Feta, Roasted Garlic and Oregano

This is a pizza for garlic lovers! Mash down the cloves as you eat – they should be soft and will have lost their pungency.

Serves 4

INGREDIENTS
1 medium garlic head, unpeeled
3 tbsp olive oil
1 medium red bell pepper, quartered and seeded
1 medium yellow bell pepper, quartered and seeded
2 plum tomatoes
1 quantity Basic or Superquick Pizza Dough
6 oz feta, crumbled
black pepper
1–2 tbsp chopped fresh oregano, to garnish

oregano

plum tomatoes

feta

olive oil

red and yellow bell peppers

garlic head

1 Preheat the oven to 425°F. Break the head of garlic into cloves, discarding the outer papery layers. Toss in 1 tbsp of the oil.

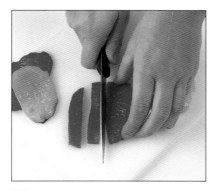

2 Place the peppers skin-side up on a baking sheet and broil until the skins are evenly charred. Place in a covered bowl for 10 minutes, then peel off the skins. Cut the flesh into strips.

3 Put the tomatoes in a bowl and pour boiling water over. Leave for 30 seconds, then plunge into cold water. Peel, seed and coarsely chop the flesh. Divide the dough into four pieces and roll out each one on a lightly floured surface to a 5 in circle.

4 Place the dough circles well apart on two greased baking sheets, then pinch up the dough edges to form a thin rim. Brush with half the remaining oil and scatter the chopped tomatoes over. Top with the peppers, crumbled feta and garlic cloves. Drizzle over the remaining oil and season with black pepper. Bake for 15–20 minutes until crisp and golden. Garnish with chopped oregano and serve immediately.

Spring Vegetable and Pine Nuts

This colorful pizza is well worth the time it takes to prepare. You can vary the ingredients according to availability.

Serves 2–3

INGREDIENTS
1 pizza base, 10–12 in diameter
3 tbsp Garlic Oil
1 quantity Tomato Sauce
4 scallions
2 zucchini
1 leek
4 oz asparagus tips
1 tbsp chopped fresh oregano
2 tbsp pine nuts
2 oz mozzarella, grated
2 tbsp freshly grated Parmesan
black pepper

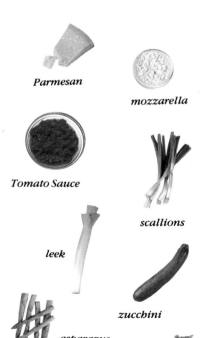

Parmesan

mozzarella

Tomato Sauce

scallions

leek

zucchini

asparagus

pine nuts

1 Preheat the oven to 425°F. Brush the pizza base with 1 tbsp of the Garlic Oil, then spread the Tomato Sauce over.

2 Slice the scallions, zucchini, leek and asparagus.

3 Heat half the remaining Garlic Oil in a frying pan and stir-fry the vegetables for 3–5 minutes.

4 Arrange the vegetables over the Tomato Sauce.

5 Sprinkle the oregano and pine nuts over the pizza.

6 Mix together the mozzarella and Parmesan and sprinkle over. Drizzle the remaining Garlic Oil over and season with black pepper. Bake for 15–20 minutes until crisp and golden. Serve immediately.

Spinach and Ricotta Panzerotti

These make great party food to serve with drinks or as tasty appetizers for a crowd.

Makes 20–24

INGREDIENTS
4 oz frozen chopped spinach,
   defrosted and squeezed dry
2 oz ricotta
2 oz freshly grated Parmesan
generous pinch freshly grated nutmeg
2 quantities Basic or Superquick Pizza
   Dough
1 egg white, lightly beaten
vegetable oil for deep-frying
salt and black pepper

ricotta

nutmeg

vegetable oil

egg

frozen spinach

Parmesan

1 Place the spinach, ricotta, Parmesan, nutmeg and seasoning in a bowl and beat until smooth.

2 Roll out the dough on a lightly floured surface to about ⅛ in thick. Using a 3 in plain round cutter stamp out 20–24 circles.

3 Spread a teaspoon of spinach mixture over one half of each circle.

4 Brush the edges of the dough with a little egg white.

5 Fold the dough over the filling and press the edges firmly together to seal.

COOK'S TIP
Do serve these as soon as possible
after frying, they will become much
less appetizing if left to cool.

6 Heat the oil in a large heavy-based
pan or deep-fat fryer to 350°F. Deep-fry
the panzerotti a few at a time for 2–3
minutes until golden. Drain on paper
towels and serve immediately.

Smoked Salmon Pizzettes

Mini pizzas topped with smoked salmon, crème fraîche and lumpfish caviar make an extra special party canapé.

Makes 10–12

INGREDIENTS
1 quantity Basic or Superquick Pizza
  Dough
1 tbsp chopped fresh chives
1 tbsp olive oil
3–4 oz smoked salmon, cut into strips
4 tbsp crème fraîche
2 tbsp black lumpfish caviar
chives, to garnish

crème fraîche

olive oil

smoked salmon

chives

black lumpfish caviar

1 Preheat the oven to 400°F. Knead the dough gently, adding the chives until evenly mixed.

2 Roll out the dough on a lightly floured surface to about ⅛ in thick. Using a 3 in plain round cutter stamp out 10–12 circles.

3 Place the bases well apart on two greased baking sheets, prick all over with a fork, then brush with the oil. Bake for 10–15 minutes until crisp and golden.

4 Arrange the smoked salmon on top, then spoon on the crème fraîche. Spoon a tiny amount of lumpfish caviar in the center and garnish with chives. Serve immediately.

Sun-dried Tomatoes, Basil and Olive Pizza Bites

This quick and easy recipe uses scone pizza dough with the addition of chopped fresh basil.

Makes 24

INGREDIENTS
18–20 fresh basil leaves
1 quantity Scone Pizza Dough
2 tbsp tomato oil (from jar of sun-dried tomatoes)
1 quantity Tomato Sauce
4 oz (drained weight) sun-dried tomatoes in oil, chopped
10 pitted black olives, chopped
2 oz mozzarella, grated
2 tbsp freshly grated Parmesan
shredded basil leaves, to garnish

mozzarella

black olives

Parmesan

Tomato Sauce

tomato oil

basil

sun-dried tomatoes

1 Preheat the oven to 425°F. Tear the basil leaves into small pieces. Add half to the scone mix before mixing to a soft dough. Set aside the remainder.

2 Knead the dough gently on a lightly floured surface until smooth. Roll out and use to line a 12 × 7 in jelly roll pan. Pinch up the edges to make a thin rim.

3 Brush the base with 1 tbsp of the tomato oil, then spread the Tomato Sauce over. Scatter the sun-dried tomatoes, olives and remaining basil over.

4 Mix together the mozzarella and Parmesan and sprinkle over. Drizzle the remaining tomato oil over. Bake for about 20 minutes. Cut lengthwise and across into 24 bite-size pieces. Garnish with extra shredded basil leaves and serve immediately.

Farmhouse Pizza

This is the ultimate party pizza. Served cut into fingers, it is ideal for a crowd.

Serves 8

INGREDIENTS
6 tbsp olive oil
8 oz mushrooms, sliced
2 quantities Basic or Superquick Pizza
    Dough
1 quantity Tomato Sauce
10 oz mozzarella, thinly sliced
4 oz paper-thin smoked ham slices
6 bottled artichoke hearts in oil,
    drained and sliced
2 oz can anchovy fillets, drained and
    halved lengthwise
10 pitted black olives, halved
2 tbsp chopped fresh oregano
3 tbsp freshly grated Parmesan
black pepper

anchovy fillets

artichoke hearts

Tomato Sauce

black olives

mushrooms

mozzarella

smoked ham

olive oil

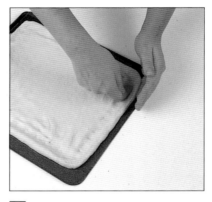

1 Preheat the oven to 425°F. Heat 2 tbsp of the oil in a large frying pan, add the mushrooms and fry for about 5 minutes until all the juices have evaporated. Leave to cool.

2 Roll out the dough on a lightly floured surface to a 12 × 10 in rectangle. Transfer to a greased baking sheet, then pinch up the dough edges to make a thin rim. Brush the dough with 2 tbsp of the oil.

3 Spread the Tomato Sauce over.

4 Arrange the sliced mozzarella over the sauce.

5 Scrunch up the ham and arrange on top with the artichoke hearts, mushrooms and anchovies.

6 Dot with the olives, then sprinkle the oregano and Parmesan over. Drizzle over the remaining oil and season with black pepper. Bake for about 25 minutes until crisp and golden. Serve immediately.

Feta, Pimiento and Pine Nut

Delight your guests with these tempting pizzas.
Substitute goat cheese for the feta if you prefer.

Makes 24

INGREDIENTS
2 quantities Basic or Superquick Pizza
   Dough
4 tbsp olive oil
2 tbsp black olive tapenade
6 oz feta
1 large canned pimiento, drained
2 tbsp chopped fresh thyme
2 tbsp pine nuts
black pepper
thyme sprigs, to garnish

pimiento

thyme

feta cheese

tapenade

pine nuts

1 Preheat the oven to 425°F. Divide the dough into 24 pieces and roll out each one on a lightly floured surface to a small oval, about ⅛ in thick. Place the ovals, well apart, on greased baking sheets and prick all over with a fork. Brush each one with 2 tbsp of the oil.

2 Spread a thin layer of the black olive tapenade on each oval and crumble the feta over.

3 Cut the pimiento into thin strips and pile on top.

4 Sprinkle each one with thyme and pine nuts. Drizzle the remaining oil over and grind over plenty of black pepper. Bake for 10–15 minutes until crisp and golden. Garnish with thyme sprigs and serve immediately.

Mozzarella, Anchovy and Pesto

These unusual pizzas combine the piquancy of olives and capers with anchovies and mozzarella.

Makes 24

INGREDIENTS
2 ready-to-cook pizza bases, about
    8 in diameter
4 tbsp olive oil
2 tbsp red pesto
12 stoned black olives
3 oz mozzarella, cubed
2 oz (drained weight) sun-dried
    tomatoes in oil, chopped
30–45/2–3 tbsp capers
2 oz can anchovy fillets, drained and
    coarsely chopped
2 tbsp freshly grated Parmesan
parsley sprigs, to garnish

parsley

sun-dried tomatoes

mozzarella

capers

olive oil

black olives

anchovy fillets

red pesto

1 Preheat the oven to 425°F. Using a 2 in plain round cutter stamp out 24 rounds from the pizza bases. Place the rounds on two greased baking sheets.

2 Brush the bases with 2 tbsp of the oil, then spread the pesto over.

3 Cut the olives into quarters lengthwise, then scatter over the bases with the mozzarella, sun-dried tomatoes, capers and anchovies.

4 Sprinkle over the Parmesan and drizzle the remaining oil over. Bake for 8–10 minutes until crisp and golden. Garnish with parsley sprigs and serve immediately.

Sun-dried Tomato Bread

This savory bread tastes delicious on its own, but it also makes exceptional sandwiches.

Makes 1 loaf

INGREDIENTS
3¼ cups bread flour
1 tsp salt
2 tsp rapid-rise dried yeast
2 oz (drained weight) sun-dried
   tomatoes in oil, chopped
¾ cup lukewarm water
5 tbsp lukewarm olive oil, plus extra
   for brushing
plain flour for dusting

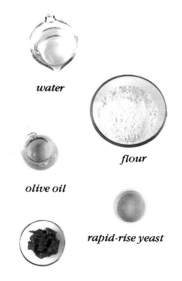

water

flour

olive oil

rapid-rise yeast

sun-dried tomatoes

salt

1 Sift the flour and salt into a large mixing bowl.

2 Stir in the yeast and sun-dried tomatoes.

3 Make a well in the center of the dry ingredients. Pour in the water and oil, and mix until the ingredients come together and form a soft dough.

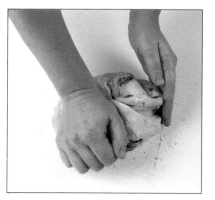

4 Turn the dough on to a lightly floured surface and knead for about 10 minutes.

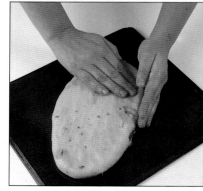

5 Shape into an oblong loaf, without making the top too smooth, and place on a greased baking sheet. Brush the top with oil, cover with plastic wrap, then let rise in a warm place for about 1 hour.

6 Meanwhile, preheat the oven to 425°F. Remove the plastic wrap, then sprinkle the top of the loaf lightly with flour. Bake for 30–40 minutes until the loaf sounds hollow when tapped on the bottom. Serve warm.

Rosemary and Sea Salt Focaccia

Focaccia is an Italian flat bread made with olive oil. Here it is given added flavor with rosemary and coarse sea salt.

Makes 1 loaf

INGREDIENTS
3 cups unbleached all-purpose
   flour
½ tsp salt
2 tsp rapid-rise dried yeast
1 cup lukewarm water
3 tbsp olive oil
1 small red onion
leaves from 1 large rosemary sprig
1 tsp coarse sea salt

coarse sea salt

water

olive oil

flour

rapid-rise yeast

red onion

rosemary

1 Sift the flour and salt into a large mixing bowl. Stir in the yeast, then make a well in the center of the dry ingredients. Pour in the water and 2 tbsp of the oil. Mix well, adding a little more water if the mixture seems dry.

2 Turn the dough on to a lightly floured surface and knead for about 10 minutes until smooth and elastic.

3 Place the dough in a greased bowl, cover and let rise in a warm place for about 1 hour until doubled in size. Punch down and knead the dough for 2–3 minutes.

4 Meanwhile, preheat the oven to 425°F. Roll out the dough to a large circle, about ½ in thick, and transfer to a greased baking sheet. Brush with the remaining oil.

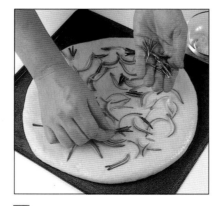

5 Halve the onion and slice into thin wedges. Sprinkle over the dough with the rosemary and sea salt, pressing in lightly.

6 Using a finger make deep indentations in the dough. Cover the surface with greased plastic wrap, then let rise in a warm place for 30 minutes. Remove the plastic wrap and bake for 25–30 minutes until golden. Serve warm.

Saffron Focaccia

A dazzling yellow bread that is light in texture and distinctive in flavor.

Makes 1 loaf

INGREDIENTS
pinch of saffron threads
²/₃ cup boiling water
2 cups flour
½ tsp salt
1 tsp easy-blend dry yeast
1 tbsp olive oil

FOR THE TOPPING
2 garlic cloves, sliced
1 red onion, cut into thin wedges
rosemary sprigs
12 black olives, pitted and coarsely
    chopped
1 tbsp olive oil

flour

garlic

rosemary

red onion

olives

saffron

yeast

1 Place the saffron in a heatproof cup and pour on the boiling water. Leave to stand and infuse until lukewarm.

2 Place the flour, salt, yeast and olive oil in a food processor. Turn on and gradually add the saffron and its liquid. Process until the dough forms into a ball.

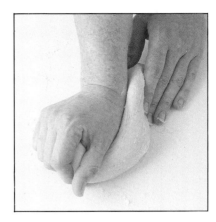

3 Turn onto a floured board and knead for 10–15 minutes. Place in a bowl, cover and leave to rise for 30–40 minutes until doubled in size.

4 Punch down the risen dough on a lightly floured surface and roll out into an oval shape, ½ in thick. Place on a lightly greased cookie sheet and leave to rise for 20–30 minutes.

5 Preheat the oven to 400°F. Press small indentations all over the surface of the focaccia with your fingers.

6 Cover with the topping ingredients, brush lightly with olive oil, and bake for 25 minutes or until the loaf sounds hollow when tapped on the bottom. Leave to cool on a wire rack.

Mini Focaccia with Pine Nuts

Pine nuts add little bites of nutty texture to these mini focaccias.

Makes 4 mini loaves

INGREDIENTS
3 cups unbleached all-purpose
    flour
½ tsp salt
2 tsp rapid-rise dried yeast
1 cup lukewarm water
3 tbsp olive oil
3–4 tbsp pine nuts
2 tsp coarse sea salt

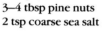
water

olive oil

rapid-rise yeast

sea salt

flour

pine nuts

1 Sift the flour and salt into a large mixing bowl. Stir in the yeast, then make a well in the center of the dry ingredients. Pour in the water and 2 tbsp of the oil. Mix well, adding more water if the mixture seems dry. Turn on to a lightly floured surface and knead for about 10 minutes until smooth and elastic. Place the dough in a greased bowl, cover and let rise in a warm place for about 1 hour until doubled in size. Punch down and knead the dough for 2–3 minutes.

2 Divide the dough into four pieces.

3 Using your hands pat out each piece on greased baking sheets to a 4 × 3 in oblong, rounded at the ends.

4 Scatter the pine nuts over and gently press them into the surface. Sprinkle with salt and brush with the remaining oil. Cover with greased plastic wrap and let rise for about 30 minutes. Meanwhile, preheat the oven to 425°F. Remove the plastic wrap and bake the focaccias for 15–20 minutes until golden. Serve warm.

Walnut Bread

The nutty flavor of this wonderfully textured bread is excellent. Try it toasted and topped with melting goat cheese for a mouthwatering snack.

Makes 2 loaves

INGREDIENTS
4 cups bread flour
2 tsp salt
2 tsp rapid-rise dried yeast
1¼ cups chopped walnuts
4 tbsp chopped fresh parsley
1⅔ cups lukewarm water
4 tbsp olive oil

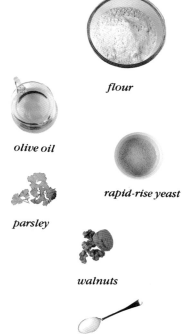

flour

olive oil

rapid-rise yeast

parsley

walnuts

salt

1 Sift the flour and salt into a large mixing bowl. Stir in the yeast, walnuts and parsley.

2 Make a well in the center of the dry ingredients. Pour in the water and oil and mix to a soft dough. Turn the dough on to a lightly floured surface and knead for about 10 minutes until smooth and elastic. Place in a greased bowl, cover and let rise in a warm place for about 1 hour until doubled in size.

3 Punch down and knead the dough for 2–3 minutes. Divide in half and shape each piece into a thick roll about 7–8 in long. Place on greased baking sheets, cover with plastic wrap and let rise for about 30 minutes.

4 Meanwhile, preheat the oven to 425°F. Remove the plastic wrap, then lightly slash the top of each loaf. Bake for 10 minutes, then reduce the oven temperature to 350°F. and bake for a further 25–30 minutes until the loaves sound hollow when tapped. Serve warm.

Olive Bread

Green olives are added to heighten the flavor of this moist bread. Use a combination of green and black olives if you prefer.

Makes 2 loaves

INGREDIENTS
6 cups bread flour
1 tsp salt
sachet of rapid-rise dried yeast
1 tbsp chopped fresh oregano
1½ cups lukewarm water
7 tbsp olive oil
about 30 stoned green olives

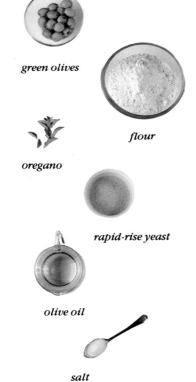

green olives

flour

oregano

rapid-rise yeast

olive oil

salt

1 Sift the flour and salt into a large mixing bowl. Stir in the yeast and oregano.

2 Measure the water into a bowl, then stir in 6 tbsp of the oil. Make a well in the center of the dry ingredients, pour in the liquid and mix to a soft dough.

3 Turn the dough on to a lightly floured surface and knead for about 10 minutes until smooth and elastic. Place in a greased bowl, cover with plastic wrap and let rise in a warm place for about 1 hour until doubled in size.

4 Punch down and knead the dough for 2–3 minutes. Divide in half, then press the dough on greased baking sheets into two ovals, about ½ in thick.

5 Using a clean finger make about 15 deep indentations over the surface of each loaf. Press an olive into each indentation.

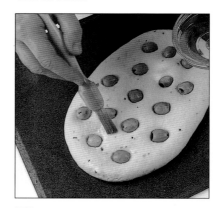

6 Brush the loaves with the remaining oil, cover with plastic wrap and let rise for 30 minutes. Meanwhile, preheat the oven to 425°F. Remove the plastic wrap and bake for 20–25 minutes until the loaves sound hollow when tapped. Serve warm.

Saffron and Basil Breadsticks

Saffron lends its delicate aroma and flavor, as well as rich yellow color, to these tasty breadsticks.

Makes 32

INGREDIENTS
generous pinch saffron strands
4 cups bread flour
1 tsp salt
2 tsp rapid-rise dried yeast
1¼ cups lukewarm water
3 tbsp olive oil
3 tbsp chopped fresh basil

flour

water

olive oil

basil

rapid-rise yeast

saffron strands

salt

1 Infuse the saffron strands in 2 tbsp hot water for 10 minutes.

2 Sift the flour and salt into a large mixing bowl. Stir in the yeast, then make a well in the center of the dry ingredients. Pour in the water and saffron liquid and start to mix a little.

3 Add the oil and basil and continue to mix to a soft dough.

4 Turn out and knead the dough on a lightly floured surface for about 10 minutes until smooth and elastic. Place in a greased bowl, cover with plastic wrap and let rise for about 1 hour until it has doubled in size.

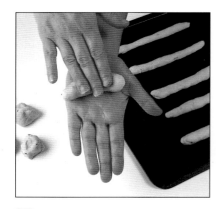

5 Punch down and knead the dough on a lightly floured surface for 2–3 minutes.

6 Preheat the oven to 425°F. Divide the dough into 32 pieces and shape into long sticks. Place well apart on greased baking sheets, then let rise for a further 15–30 minutes until they become puffy. Bake for about 15 minutes until crisp and golden. Serve warm.

INDEX